HBR Guide to
Motivating People

Harvard Business Review Guides

Arm yourself with the advice you need to succeed on the job, from the most trusted brand in business. Packed with how-to essentials from leading experts, the HBR Guides provide smart answers to your most pressing work challenges.

The titles include:

HBR Guide to Being More Productive

HBR Guide to Better Business Writing

HBR Guide to Building Your Business Case

HBR Guide to Buying a Small Business

HBR Guide to Coaching Employees

HBR Guide to Data Analytics Basics for Managers

HBR Guide to Delivering Effective Feedback

HBR Guide to Emotional Intelligence

HBR Guide to Finance Basics for Managers

HBR Guide to Getting the Right Work Done

HBR Guide to Leading Teams

HBR Guide to Making Every Meeting Matter

HBR Guide to Managing Stress at Work

HBR Guide to Managing Up and Across

HBR Guide to Negotiating

HBR Guide to Office Politics

HBR Guide to Performance Management

HBR Guide to Persuasive Presentations

HBR Guide to Project Management

HBR Guide to
Motivating
People

HARVARD BUSINESS REVIEW PRESS

Boston, Massachusetts

Copyright 2019 Harvard Business School Publishing Corporation

Printed in the United States of America

10 9 8 7 6 5 4 3 2 1

The web addresses referenced in this book were live and correct at the time of the book's publication but may be subject to change.

Library of Congress Cataloging-in-Publication data is forthcoming.

ISBN: 978-1-63369-676-1

eISBN: 978-1-63369-677-8

The paper used in this publication meets the requirements of the American National Standard for Permanence of Paper for Publications and Documents in Libraries and Archives Z39.48-1992

What You'll Learn

When people are inspired to do their best every day, they're more creative, collaborative, productive, and satisfied. They come to work with energy and ideas, and even the most audacious goals seem attainable. But when engagement is low, or enthusiasm and buy-in are lacking, it's an uphill battle to make progress toward even the simplest objectives. If your team isn't happy then neither are you—and if things don't improve soon *your* job may be at risk.

So how do you get people more engaged? If your company is like most, HR may conduct annual surveys and roll out flex work arrangements, free snacks, or other perks to maintain morale. But motivation isn't that simple—and it certainly doesn't look the same for everyone. As a manager, you shape people's daily work experience. You have the opportunity to discover what makes them tick. What are their talents? Their values? Their goals? If you can unlock the passion and potential of every person on your team, they will choose to give 110%. And when that happens, everyone wins.

This guide will help you:

- Identify, leverage, and celebrate everyone's unique strengths

- Ask the right questions to find out why someone isn't engaged—and what you can do to help

- Tap into the psychological drives that ignite top performance

- Coach people as they develop the skills they need to thrive

- Inspire everyone to go above and beyond their job descriptions

- Decide when it's time to push new challenges and stretch assignments

- Prevent healthy engagement from slipping into overwork and burnout—especially among your stars

- Connect employees to the higher purpose of their work

- Create a positive team culture to unleash productivity throughout the organization

- Embrace the job of motivating employees as a key to everyone's success

Contents

Introduction: Why Motivation Is a Manager's Job   1

*You can inspire people to bring their best
selves to work.*

    BY SUSAN DAVID

SECTION ONE

Assess Engagement on Your Team

   1. **Want to Know How Engaged People Are?
Here's What to Measure**   11

    *Look beyond annual surveys to discretionary
effort, relationships, and schedule.*

    BY RYAN FULLER

  2. **Where Engagement Surveys Go Wrong**   21

    *Strategies for avoiding common biases when
crafting questions.*

    BY JENNIFER CULLEN

  3. **Go Ahead: Ask Your Employees If
They're Happy**   27

    *One-on-one conversations will help you
retain and engage them.*

    BY ALLISON RIMM

Contents

SECTION TWO

Understand Common Motivators

4. It Takes More Than Just Extrinsic Rewards
   to Inspire People   35

   *Financial incentives often do more harm
   than good.*

5. What Maslow Got Wrong About Our
   Psychological Needs   47

   *Satisfy people's deepest needs—for
   autonomy, relatedness, and competence.*

   BY SUSAN FOWLER

6. A Recipe for Disengagement on Your Team   53

   *Stop the drive-by praise and guilt
   gratitude—people see through it.*

   BY RON CARUCCI

7. Motivating Salespeople: What Really Works   59

   *Tailor rewards to your stars, laggards,
   and core performers.*

   BY THOMAS STEENBURGH AND MICHAEL AHEARNE

8. One Engagement Strategy Does Not Fit All   71

   Find out what makes each person tick.

   BY NATALIE BAUMGARTNER

SECTION THREE

Make Work More Meaningful

9. The Power of Small Wins   79

   *Making progress possible boosts creativity
   and productivity.*

   BY TERESA AMABILE AND STEVE KRAMER

10. **The Best Leaders Show People That Their Work Matters**   105

Cultivate the four characteristics that set master motivators apart.

BY LEWIS GARRAD AND TOMAS CHAMORRO-PREMUZIC

11. **Great Storytelling Connects Employees to Their Work**   111

Get people to see past a task to the service they're providing others.

BY JOSEPH GRENNY

12. **Help Someone Discover Work That Excites Them**   119

Unlock passion, commitment, and performance with these questions.

BY AMY JEN SU

13. **How to Motivate Employees to Go Beyond Their Jobs**   125

Let them choose when and how they volunteer extra effort.

BY MARK C. BOLINO AND ANTHONY C. KLOTZ

SECTION FOUR

Encourage Growth and Development

14. **To Support Learning, Managers Need to Coach**   133

Five tips for guiding others along the road to peak performance.

BY MONIQUE VALCOUR

Contents

15. Why Talented People Don't Use
    Their Strengths   139
    *Identify their superpowers—and then put
    those skills to work.*

    BY WHITNEY JOHNSON

16. Let Employees Personalize Their Jobs   145
    Fit jobs to people, instead of people to jobs.

    BY VIVEK BAPAT

17. Mentoring Someone Who Doesn't Know
    What Their Career Goals Should Be   155
    *Encourage them to develop transferable
    skills while they test different paths.*

    BY TANIA LUNA AND JORDAN COHEN

18. How to Retain and Engage Your B Players   161
    *Uncover hidden strengths, conquer limiting
    beliefs, and give permission to shine.*

    BY LIZ KISLIK

19. What to Do When a Good Employee Stops
    Trying to Grow   167
    If they're stagnating, it's time for a change.

    BY WHITNEY JOHNSON

SECTION FIVE

Prevent Burnout on Your Team

20. One in Five Highly Engaged Employees
    Is at Risk of Burnout   175
    *You may be in danger of losing your most
    motivated, hardworking people.*

    BY EMMA SEPPALA AND JULIA MOELLER

21. **Your Overworked, Stressed-Out Team Needs Relief**   185

Focus everyone on the work that matters by clarifying team purpose.

BY JULIE MOSOW

22. **How to Apply the Right Amount of Pressure**   195

Capture the benefits of productive stress by turning the heat up or down.

BY LIANE DAVEY

23. **Burnout at Work Isn't Just About Exhaustion. It's Also About Loneliness**   203

Foster compassion, strong networks, and solidarity so people feel less alone.

BY EMMA SEPPALA AND MARISSA KING

24. **Don't Let Grunt Work Drag Down Performance**   209

Everyone has to do it, but your team shouldn't feel trapped by it.

BY WHITNEY JOHNSON

SECTION SIX

Create a Culture of Engagement

25. **Positive Work Cultures Are More Productive**   217

Support six key qualities on your team to build a healthier, happier company.

BY EMMA SEPPALA AND KIM CAMERON

26. **Flex Work Doesn't Help Employees If It Hurts Their Careers**   225

Make sure people feel safe using the benefits you offer.

BY LINDSEY TRIMBLE O'CONNOR AND ERIN CECH

Contents

27. Rules for Designing an Inspiring Workplace   233

Environmental psychology points the way to better spaces for all.

BY SALLY AUGUSTIN

28. IDEO's Engagement Formula   241

Four principles that powered the innovator's success.

BY DUANE BRAY

Index   247

Why Motivation Is a Manager's Job

by Susan David

We need to talk about motivation. While every workplace has its share of employees who are just punching the clock, the problem is much more troubling than many imagine. In fact, the latest iteration (2017) of Gallup's "State of the American Workplace" report shows dismal engagement levels among workers, and the numbers are barely budging. Between the 2017 report and the previous one, published in 2013, engagement held at around 30 percent in the United States and 13 percent globally. This means that nearly nine out of ten people are not engaged at work, a situation Gallup researchers refer to as a "crisis in employee engagement."

Calling this a crisis is no hyperbole. When compared to business units in Gallup's top quartile for engagement, business units in the bottom quartile have 37% higher absenteeism, 45% more accidents, 16% lower profitability, and a 65% lower share price over time, while those in the top quartile outperform those in the bottom on these metrics and also have lower turnover (24% in high-turnover companies and 59% in low turnover companies), 10% higher customer satisfaction, 17% higher productivity, and 20% higher sales.

Employee engagement has been so convincingly tied to productivity, creativity, collaboration, and individual and organizational performance that a whole industry has emerged to help companies track and sustain or improve it. Billions are spent every year to pinpoint the problem using surveys and to find a magic formula for solving it with fancy perks, office redesigns, managerial checklists, and other companywide initiatives.

The irony is that these efforts can be disengaging. I once sat in on a meeting at a company struggling with low engagement in which one of the senior leaders in the room actually said, "We have to mandate that every manager have at least one authentic conversation per month." How the company planned to measure and enforce that, I have no idea. This goes to show that many policies come from a poor understanding of how motivation really works—in spite of good intentions.

Where do we go wrong? One of the great myths of employee engagement is that it's just about getting more from your people, getting them to work longer and harder for the good of the organization at the expense of the employees themselves. However, the research doesn't support this.

Through years of research and experience as a psychologist working in organizations, I've come to see engagement as a condition in which people are enabled to bring the best of themselves to the workplace. When they can do this—when they feel seen, that they belong, that they are learning but also developing mastery—it has a profound impact on the organization, yes, but also on employees as individuals. This sense of connectedness with one's job has a predictive, positive effect on well-being and resilience and can decrease stress and anxiety. Feeling less connected to our work, on the other hand—going through the motions—is tied to burnout and has negative implications for people's personal and professional relationships and home lives.

When the spark of engagement is ignited in people, everyone wins. But, as my research has shown, and as many experts in this guide will argue, all the free meals, ping pong tables, required company fun, and unlimited vacation and flextime policies are no match for the power of getting to know someone on a personal level and discovering how to help that person bring their best self to work. Engagement can't be written into a job description. It can't be mandated and it can't be bought or coerced. It's entirely at the employee's discretion—it's theirs to give or not. And this is where managers come in.

I believe that engagement should be everyone's responsibility: the individual employee's, the manager's, and the organization's. But the organization can only control what I call hygiene factors—the baseline elements of a job, such as salary, benefits, organizational strategy, and overall working environment, all of which are essential to attracting and retaining talent but which do not lead to true engagement on their own.

It is managers who have the biggest impact on engagement or disengagement, because they interact with their employees and shape their work experience daily. So managers have a remarkable opportunity to connect and inspire. Engagement is, after all, a human, relational exchange rather than a transactional one—in the same way that good parenting is not just about making sure you're feeding your children and meeting their basic needs. It's also about wanting them to thrive.

But managers have a lot on their plates, and increasing employee engagement can feel like it's just another task to cross off their list, especially if improving numbers quickly is mandated from above. When motivation is approached as a have-to goal, managers' efforts at recognition, praise, and gratitude ring hollow and can even cause resentment (as you'll read in chapter 6, "A Recipe for Disengagement on Your Team," by Ron Carucci).

Ultimately, it will be easier to get *your* work done if your team is willing to go the extra mile. And the rewards don't end there. In an environment where managers lack control over budget, workload, pay and perks, and other aspects of the work experience, motivation costs nothing. Learning how to engage people and unlock their full potential will also make you a better manager. More importantly, it will make work meaningful for everyone involved.

So where to begin? The bad news is that human behavior is complex, and there is no simple formula for engagement. The good news is that this guide can help. If you want to engage your team and improve all kinds of other metrics in the process, first remember that engagement is not something that you can do *to* people. It's a context that you create in which people are inspired to bring their best and full selves to work. Start with these two steps:

Step 1: Understand the Research

Motivation may not be straightforward, but there is a wealth of research out there (some covered in the pages of this book) that has yielded important frameworks and practical advice you can start using today. In my experience looking across psychological traditions, four key sources of motivation rise to the surface:

1. **A sense of team and belonging:** In order for people to be their best at work, to feel that there's space for them and that their voices are heard, they need psychological safety. Everyone wants to feel that they can bring their emotional truth to the workplace, and also that they are a part of something bigger than themselves or the specific task at hand. That's why it's crucial for managers not only to get to know their direct reports, but to create a shared sense of "why" on their team.

2. **Autonomy:** People want the power to shape their environments and make choices and decisions for themselves. The more managers can avoid micromanaging and empower their people instead, the better.

3. **Flexibility:** Employees want to feel that there is a give and take within the organization. Demonstrate flexibility in terms of how and where work is done. And if people want to try something new, give them some leeway, even if it means diverging from the normal course of business.

4. **Stimulating work:** There are risks associated with extremes on both ends of this spectrum. If someone is either over-challenged or over-competent in their job, there's a good chance they will become disengaged. Striking a balance between challenging people to learn and grow and also giving them opportunities to use their strengths can help mitigate the risks.

Step 2: Take an Individualized Approach

Once you have a grasp on the research, you must get to know each person on your team. We are wonderfully unique (as Natalie Baumgartner explains in chapter 8, "One Engagement Strategy Does Not Fit All"), so what gets me out of bed in the morning is likely to be different than what stirs you to action. Motivation may be everyone's job, but as we discussed, you, the manager, are in the best position to help people understand their core drives and support them on their journey to thriving at work. Find out what engages *your* employees—not someone else's.

In the following chapters, you'll hear from many experts in the field on all of the stages of this engagement journey. First, you'll need to assess engagement levels on your team, which we cover in section 1. Are you asking the right questions? Are you having one-on-one conversations with everyone on your team or are you leaving measurement entirely up to company surveys? In section 2 we'll look at more research on what motivates people to give their best. Do people value extrinsic rewards? Or is meeting psychological needs more important?

In section 3 we explore proven strategies for addressing engagement issues on your team and making work more meaningful. How do you plan to show people that their work matters? How can you tap into their passions and encourage them to go above and beyond the call of duty? In section 4 you'll learn how to support people's growth and development. Are you coaching employees, helping them identify and use their unique strengths?

In section 5 we cover burnout—the dark side of engagement. Are you protecting people from overdoing it, especially those who are deeply engaged? How can you help people manage heavy workloads and minimize unproductive stress while harnessing the positive stress that can drive breakthrough performance? And finally, section 6 looks at how to create a culture of engagement. Culture might seem like an element of work life over which managers have little influence. But many of the strategies described here start at the team level or have important implications for how you manage direct reports.

If I had to emphasize one piece of advice for managers trying to create the conditions for engagement, it would be first and foremost to establish a shared sense of meaning on your team. The organizational environment will not always support your efforts to motivate your employees, and it may sometimes seem to be working against you. But even though you can't control every aspect of your team's work experience, you *can* collectively answer the questions, "What do we want to be as a team?" "What are our shared values?" "How do we want to treat one another?" Establishing a shared "why" is enormously powerful and will bring people together with strength and clarity, even in a context that is challenging and imperfect. Being part of a strong team taps into a lot of the sources of motivation that we've discussed, including instilling a sense of belonging, making work meaningful, contributing to a larger purpose, and building a culture of engagement.

The psychology of motivation is complicated: You may never reach a point where you'll be able to say, "Everyone is engaged—my work here is done!" Have compassion for yourself as you take on the difficult but essential work of engaging people. Remind yourself why you're doing this—what personal values are you fulfilling? Simply seeing motivation as an important part of your role rather than something you must do out of obligation means your heart is in the right place. Armed with the research and the strategies in this book, I think you'll find that your efforts will be rewarded many times over—not only in your team's engagement but also in your own.

Assess Engagement on Your Team

CHAPTER 1

Want to Know How Engaged People Are? Here's What to Measure

by Ryan Fuller

Much has been studied about the impact of employee engagement on company performance, and there is general agreement that increased engagement drives results: Gallup, for example, suggests a 20% or better boost to productivity and profitability for companies with high engagement.[1] Such companies, however, may be few and far between: Gallup also reports that only

---

Adapted from "A Primer on Measuring Employee Engagement" on hbr.org, November 17, 2014 (product #H0123Z).

30% of American workers, and 13% of global workers, are engaged in their jobs.

Taken together, it's easy to see why so many companies are talking about it and making it a priority. But when you look at how engagement gets measured, that's where things start to break down a bit.

The typical approach is an annual engagement survey where employees are effectively asked, through various types of questions, to rate their own level of engagement. Assuming honest survey responses, this approach provides good input into the employee attitude side of the equation (for example, how engaged they perceive themselves to be), but unfortunately it doesn't do a good job of gathering objective data on just how engaged employees actually are (for example, discretionary effort). While knowing what employees think certainly has value, this data suffers from the same challenges of any other survey-based effort: it becomes dated quickly, there's availability bias from respondents thinking of only recent events, and potentially gamed results—people telling you what they think you want to hear rather than what they really think.

The field of people analytics is opening the door to much better data, and there are more direct measures for companies trying to better understand engagement levels. A company might begin by analyzing the following:

- **The amount of work that occurs outside of normal working hours (evenings and weekends).** This is a good indicator of discretionary effort.

- **The number of network connections and time spent with people outside of immediate team or region.** Building broad networks beyond the core team is a sign of high engagement.

- **The percentage of participation in ad hoc meetings and initiatives vs. recurring meetings and processes.** Participation in only highly structured events can be an indicator of low engagement.

- **Time spent collaborating directly with customers outside of normal scope of work.** This and other measures like it can indicate people are highly engaged enough to help their colleagues even though they might not get credit for it.

This approach allows you to measure *actual* engagement rather than *self-perceived* engagement. Further, you can deploy a number of additional metrics to understand what may actually be driving these engagement levels. Some metrics we have found to be valuable are:

Management quality and time investment, which can consist of:

- Time spent in one-on-ones with a manager per week. Engagement typically increases as an individual gets more time with his or her boss.

- Time spent in the presence of skip-level leadership. Engagement can increase as people get more exposure to colleagues up the ladder.

- Quality and breadth of a manager's network. Engagement often increases in people who have well-connected direct managers.

- The percentage of a manager's time spent with the team. A number that's too low or too high typically decreases engagement.

Influence from colleagues—because the engagement level of colleagues is infectious—including:

- The ratio of highly engaged employees to unengaged on a team.

- The ratio of highly engaged employees to unengaged among a person's most frequent co-collaborators.

Relationships:

- The number of strong-tie connections, defined as strong relationships characterized by frequent and relatively intimate interactions. Engagement typically increases as people have more, and stronger, relationships.

- The number of weak-tie connections, which are infrequent interactions with people outside of an individual's core working team. Engagement typically increases as people are exposed to ideas from beyond their core relationships.

- Variability of network over time, or the extent to which an individual's core network fluctuates month over month. Very high variability can indicate a rapid change in role and be unsettling for employees, while very low variability can indicate someone stagnating.

Work schedule:

- Hours per week spent in meetings with more than 20 attendees. Not surprisingly, engagement typically decreases the more time people spend in very large group settings where it is hard to be much more than an audience member.

- Calendar fragmentation, which is when people don't have enough time—generally about two hours—to work between meetings and other events. Engagement typically decreases when people's schedules are overly fragmented.

When this information is paired with traditional attitudinal data such as satisfaction scores, pulse surveys, or annual survey-driven engagement measures, they come together to give an even more accurate picture of what engagement truly means—and where your company is falling short. You can then monitor changes in the data in the form of anonymized dashboard tools, often in real time, or it can be shared transparently with employees so they have a better context for engagement and how they compare with their colleagues in aggregate.

Through my work at VoloMetrix, I've seen firsthand the results that measuring employee engagement can have on firms. One company with an extraordinary talent shortage ran a study with several quarters of anonymized voluntary attrition data in combination with a number of people analytics metrics to see if there was a correlation. The results were staggering. You could literally see a steady week-by-week change in behaviors for employees starting a full 52 weeks in advance of the moment they quit. With very high correlations, these

13 SIGNS THAT SOMEONE IS ABOUT TO QUIT, ACCORDING TO RESEARCH

by Timothy M. Gardner and Peter W. Hom

To help managers and companies identify employees at risk of quitting, we investigated whether people exhibit certain cues before giving notice. We uncovered a set of behavioral changes—what we dub pre-quitting behaviors—that are strong predictors of voluntary quits in the 12 months after being observed by managers. Out of a list of 900 possible behaviors, we narrowed the list down to 13:

1. Their work productivity has decreased more than usual.

2. They have acted less like a team player than usual.

3. They have been doing the minimum amount of work more frequently than usual.

4. They have been less interested in pleasing their manager than usual.

employees were spending less time interacting with people outside of their department or region, less time in ad hoc interactions, and less time being active outside of normal working hours, among other things. What this data makes clear is that the majority of these employees hadn't decided to quit a year in advance; rather, their

5. They have been less willing to commit to long-term timelines than usual.

6. They have exhibited a negative change in attitude.

7. They have exhibited less effort and work motivation than usual.

8. They have exhibited less focus on job-related matters than usual.

9. They have expressed dissatisfaction with their current job more frequently than usual.

10. They have expressed dissatisfaction with their supervisor more frequently than usual.

11. They have left early from work more frequently than usual.

12. They have lost enthusiasm for the mission of the organization.

(continued)

13 SIGNS THAT SOMEONE IS ABOUT TO QUIT, ACCORDING TO RESEARCH

13. They have shown less interest in working with customers than usual.

Once the 13 pre-quitting behaviors had been identified, they were put to the test in a cross-company survey. The more an employee behaved in these ways, the more likely they were to quit.

What should you do if you detect these behaviors in one of your own? Invest in retaining star employees at risk of leaving in the short-term. You can also try "stay interviews": Instead of conducting only exit interviews to learn what caused good employees to quit, hold regular one-on-one conversations with high performers to learn what keeps them working in your organization and what could be changed to keep them from straying.

Timothy M. Gardner is an associate professor of management at the Jon M. Huntsman School of Business at Utah State University. **Peter W. Hom** is a professor of management at the W. P. Carey School of Business at Arizona State University.

Adapted from content posted on hbr.org, October 20, 2016 (product #H037NY).

engagement levels started dropping . . . and dropping . . . and dropping . . . until they got to the point where they realized it was time to quit. (See the sidebar, "13 Signs That Someone Is About to Quit, According to Research" for more on the behaviors to watch for.) With this information in hand, the company started measuring engagement and providing feedback to managers with plenty of time to make appropriate adjustments to retain their top people.

There are many factors that contribute to employee engagement—ranging from corporate culture to management style to competing priorities outside of work—and the pertinent factors are different for each employee. This complexity is what makes it so challenging to measure and understand engagement in an actionable way. While still in its infancy, people analytics is beginning to give organizations the data and tools to understand what drives engagement, perhaps even better than employees understand themselves. Qualitative data from Gallup's engagement survey and others like it has been sufficient to prove the case for greater investment. Now, with the ability to directly measure engagement, there is no telling what organizations and employees themselves will learn about what drives them.

———————

Ryan Fuller is the CEO and cofounder of VoloMetrix, a leading people analytics company acquired by Microsoft in 2015. At Microsoft, Ryan leads the workplace analytics and MyAnalytics product teams within Office 365 focused on transforming organizational productivity and employee experience.

NOTE

1. Susan Sorenson, "How Employee Engagement Drives Growth," Gallup Workplace, June 20, 2013, http://www.gallup.com/business journal/163130/employee-engagement-drives-growth.aspx.

CHAPTER 2

Where Engagement Surveys Go Wrong

by Jennifer Cullen

Many organizations conduct surveys to gain insight into levels of satisfaction, burnout, and engagement among employees. But serious flaws in how those surveys are designed often lead to bad results. Well-intentioned leaders, following an inaccurate roadmap of where the problems lie, end up wasting time, energy, and resources on the wrong things. For example, they may ask people if overwork is an issue and then try to reduce the load, when the real problem is more psychological.

Adapted from "Where Employee Surveys on Burnout and Engagement Go Wrong" on hbr.org, December 14, 2017 (product #H042FW).

The answer is not to do away with surveys entirely—they are still a valuable way to learn about employees' feelings and experiences and to identify challenges that make it tougher for them to do their jobs, such as a lack of support from managers, a lack of confidence in teammates, and daily work that doesn't line up with their own values and goals.

The solution is to design better surveys. If you want to help employees feel more connected and committed to the organization and motivated by the work they're doing, start with questionnaires that will assess engagement accurately, without falling prey to the psychological hurdles that skew results. Here are two of the biggest culprits:

Social Desirability Bias

When employees are asked to complete surveys, their responses can be shaped by social desirability bias—the impulse to present themselves in a positive light so their bosses will think well of them. The survey becomes an exercise in "impression management" rather than a tool for change, because respondents don't want to suggest that they personally have a problem or can't handle their work. Even when workplace surveys are administered by third parties, as they often are, studies have found that anonymity does not completely erase the social desirability response bias.[1] That's in part because people don't want to think of *themselves* in a negative light.

If you ask them to respond to a statement such as "I feel overworked" or "I feel burned out," they're more likely to say no than yes. It puts the focus on them and their feelings, rather than how the organization or the work is structured. It's better to ask them to respond to a statement like this: "Generally, I believe my workload is reasonable for my role." That way, people are assessing the firm or the role, not themselves.

Similarly, I've found that "we" questions can be more effective than "I" questions. For example, you might ask employees to rate the accuracy of this statement: "We are encouraged to be innovative even though some of our initiatives may not succeed." By referring to "our initiatives" rather than "my initiatives," you can remove judgment about the individual from the equation—and elicit more candor.

Acquiescence Bias

The other psychological hurdle is the tendency to say we agree as a default response to survey statements, particularly when our knowledge is limited or none of the available answers fit.[2]

Consider this example: Some organizations ask people whether the executives are great role models for employees. But many employees don't have enough access to the executive team to form an accurate judgment. If that's not one of the options in the survey, people who feel that way may simply select "agree" or choose a "neutral" response. And that's not telling you anything meaningful about role modeling in the organization.

Those psychological factors aside, here are two other flaws to look for in workplace survey design:

Double-Barrel Questions

I see these frequently. They're statements with two components that may be totally unrelated, such as "I am motivated to perform my best work and we are good at holding people accountable." Those are separate observations; one doesn't hinge on the other. So people should be asked to respond to two distinct statements: "I am motivated to perform my best work in this organization" and "We hold ourselves and our team members accountable for results."

Ambiguity

Sometimes questions are downright confusing because they're indirect. For instance, surveys may ask "Do you have a best friend at work?" in an effort to measure how much employees enjoy being there. But that question can mean different things to different people. Is it asking whether you've chosen someone to be your "best friend at work"? Or whether one of your best friends in the world happens to be a colleague? Also, some people have one or two "best friends," while others have a dozen or more. And the response won't give managers any clear or actionable information. After all, you can have a best friend at work and still be disengaged and burned out.

Other sources of ambiguity include double negatives that leave people unsure what the question even is ("I don't feel that my company fails to provide adequate resources to enable me to do my job") and rating systems that switch directions partway through (where "5" means something positive, then something negative).

By addressing these flaws in survey design and asking questions that give employees the freedom, clarity, and psychological safety they need to be fully honest, organizations and managers can get more accurate results and identify the right problems to fix. But even then, there's another pitfall to watch out for. In hopes of gathering as much information as possible, some companies make engagement surveys mandatory or offer incentives for participation. I always discourage that.

Explain to employees why their responses are important, and then see what happens. If participation is particularly low in one unit and high in another, that can be a sign that certain parts of the company are engaged while others are not. Whether an employee chooses to participate is, in itself, an important piece of feedback.

Jennifer Cullen is an industrial/organizational psychologist and a director of people science at Culture Amp.

NOTES

1. Yphtach Lelkes et al., "Complete Anonymity Compromises the Accuracy of Self-Reports," *Journal of Experimental Social Psychology* 48, no. 6 (2012): 1291–1299.

2. Willem E. Saris, Jon A. Krosnick, Melanie Revilla, and Eric M. Shaeffer, "Comparing Questions with Agree/Disagree Response Options to Questions with Item-Specific Response Options," *Survey Research Methods* 4 (2010): 61–79.

CHAPTER 3

Go Ahead: Ask Your Employees If They're Happy

by Allison Rimm

When was the last time you made the effort to learn, *really* learn, what the people you work with are thinking and how they're feeling about their jobs? With Gallup's 2017 State of the American Workplace survey showing that 70% of U.S. employees are not engaged at work, it seems that the majority of managers would greet that question with a blank stare. Those managers are missing key information needed to attract and retain talented staff—not to mention keep them actively engaged in turning out superior results.

Adapted from content posted on hbr.org, September 18, 2013 (product #H00DVZ).

Despite the dismal statistics on workplace engagement, there are many enlightened leaders who do one simple thing: They ask their employees how they feel. When they do so, they receive priceless information that helps them retain their best employees and optimize their productivity.

Daniel Parent, director of field human resources at video game retailer GameStop, is one of those leaders. He knows the power of checking in with his team. He has a recurring appointment on his schedule that says, "Ask employees how happy they are at work and what I can do to make them happier." Daniel has learned over the years that simply asking these two questions indicates to his group that they have his support. Furthermore, he learns what their real issues are so he can provide them with meaningful direction.

By knowing what motivates his team, he can help boost their performance *and* their satisfaction on the job. His questioning also serves as an early warning system, allowing him to head off issues before they become intractable problems. Take Jennifer, for example. She so desperately wanted to be a good employee that she struggled in her new role as a working mother. Daniel recalled his conversation with her shortly after she returned to work from her maternity leave as one of the most poignant he'd ever had. When he asked Jennifer how happy she was at work, she confessed that trying to juggle both roles left her feeling like she wasn't a good person.

Getting permission from her boss to spend time with her new baby was what made the difference for Jennifer. She and Daniel worked out an arrangement that met both of their needs. By communicating regularly, Daniel was able to reassure Jennifer that she was meeting all of his expectations and then some. That allowed her to turn her full attention to her child outside of work and really enjoy their time together. "I would never have known this was bothering her if I didn't ask," he says.

Daniel also recounts another instance in which an employee put what she perceived to be the needs of the company above her personal well-being. Heading into a meeting, she told him that she had a dentist appointment and would have to leave promptly at 4 p.m. when the meeting ended. At 4:10, the meeting was still in high gear with no sign of ending. Daniel leaned over to his colleague and whispered that she'd better leave in order to make her appointment. With a grateful smile, she slipped out and took care of her teeth.

Daniel points out that people don't work for a company; they work for their boss. He has had employees tell him that they stay at GameStop because of him. "These are talented people who could easily get another, better-paying job elsewhere." The small investment of time he makes in asking his employees how happy they are has paid off many times over when he considers what it would cost to replace any member of his team.

Assuming your team is made up of high-performing, highly motivated individuals whom you want to retain, here's an action plan for monitoring and improving their engagement:

- Put a recurring appointment—monthly or quarterly—on your calendar and ask your employees whether they are happy at work and what you can do to make them happier. Don't wait for the annual review to have this conversation.

- Maintain open lines of communication so that you can offer support and address issues before they become full-blown problems.

- Help all team members manage their professional obligations so they can meet their personal needs, allowing them to be present and focused on their work when they are in the office.

- Keep questioning. Don't assume that you have all the information you need if you've asked people once whether they're happy. Circumstances inside and outside of the workplace change over time, and feelings can evolve accordingly.

Remember, relationships are built on a series of little moments that create big impact over time. Sending someone gratefully off to the dentist is not an earth-shattering event on its own. But it is an affirmation that someone's personal needs are important and to be honored. Taken as a whole, many small actions can strengthen someone's foundation or weaken it. The Gallup survey suggests that there is more erosion than building of the human spirit happening in the American workplace. Be someone who builds others up rather than tears them down. Little things matter in a big way.

As Daniel says, checking in with his employees like this is all about retention. By communicating regularly with his employees, he knows what motivates them and the challenges they need to overcome in order to do their best work. This knowledge helps him reward his most talented team members in ways that are meaningful to them, which can change over time, depending on what is happening in both their personal and professional lives. Daniel's efforts have been rewarded in the form of a highly engaged, productive and, yes, happy team of employees.

———————————

Allison Rimm is a management consultant, speaker, and executive coach devoted to nurturing a positive, productive workplace. She is the former senior vice president for strategic planning and information management at Massachusetts General Hospital and best-selling author of *The Joy of Strategy: A Business Plan for Life*.

Understand Common Motivators

CHAPTER 4

It Takes More Than Just Extrinsic Rewards to Inspire People

When people think about how to motivate employees, it's often external rewards like pay hikes, promotions, prizes, or bonuses that come immediately to mind. But managers have a lot more tools at their disposal. In fact, research shows that intrinsic rewards are generally more effective at sustaining high performance and engagement—and are fortuitously under a manager's control. Let's take a closer look at why motivating with money might not be the best strategy.

Adapted from *HBR Guide to Performance Management* (product #10119), Harvard Business Review Press, 2017.

Extrinsic Rewards

External, tangible forms of recognition are often the first course of action when the troops are flagging. On the surface, extrinsic rewards tend to be easy to execute: "If you make your quota, we'll pay you $5,000." In fact, most organizations' established reward systems are built around extrinsic rewards, and in some instances, they are effective, particularly in industries like sales, where bonuses can be linked to reaching certain quantitative goals. (See chapter 7 for more on how to reward sales-people effectively.)

But many managers disagree with the notion that financial incentives are necessary to boost performance. Extrinsic rewards don't necessarily make people work harder or better. As Alfie Kohn writes in his widely cited HBR article, "Why Incentive Plans Cannot Work," "rewards typically undermine the very processes they are intended to enhance."

When such motivators do succeed, the positive effects are often short-lived. Money matters, certainly, and an organization will have a tough time recruiting and keeping good employees without a competitive level of pay and benefits. (As you can see from the sidebar, "The Most Desirable Employee Benefits," quality health care, flexible hours, generous vacation policies, and work-from-home options top the list.)

But while money can be a motivator, it does not build commitment and can also encourage the wrong behaviors, such as cutting ethical corners to earn a bonus or to game the reward system. And tensions can run high when monetary prizes are awarded for the results of a

THE MOST DESIRABLE EMPLOYEE BENEFITS

by Kerry Jones

In today's hiring market, a generous benefits package is essential for attracting and retaining top talent. According to Glassdoor's 2015 Employment Confidence Survey, about 60% of people report that benefits and perks are a major factor in considering whether to accept a job offer. The survey also found that 80% of employees would choose additional benefits over a pay raise.

Google is famous for its over-the-top perks, which include lunches made by a professional chef, biweekly chair massages, yoga classes, and haircuts. Twitter employees enjoy three catered meals per day, on-site acupuncture, and improv classes. SAS has a college scholarship program for the children of employees. And plenty of smaller companies have received attention for their unusual benefits, such as vacation expense reimbursement (at Moz) and free books (at Buffer).

But what should a business do if it can't afford Google-sized benefits? You don't need to break the bank to offer attractive extras. A new study on employee benefits conducted by my team at Fractl found that, after health insurance, employees place the highest value on benefits that are relatively low-cost to employers, such as flexible hours, more paid vacation time, and work-from-home options. Furthermore, we found that certain benefits can win over some job

(continued)

THE MOST DESIRABLE EMPLOYEE BENEFITS

seekers faced with higher-paying offers that come with fewer additional advantages.

As part of our study, we gave 2,000 U.S. workers, ranging in age from 18 to 81, a list of 17 benefits and asked them how heavily they would weigh the options when deciding between a high-paying job and a lower-paying job with more perks (figure 4-1).

FIGURE 4-1

Which benefits are most valued by job seekers?

When choosing between a high-paying job and a lower-paying one with better benefits, respondents said health insurance and flexible hours might tip them toward the latter.

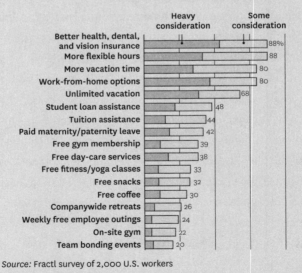

Percentage of respondents who said the benefit would be taken into consideration

Benefit	Percentage
Better health, dental, and vision insurance	88%
More flexible hours	88
More vacation time	80
Work-from-home options	80
Unlimited vacation	68
Student loan assistance	48
Tuition assistance	44
Paid maternity/paternity leave	42
Free gym membership	39
Free day-care services	38
Free fitness/yoga classes	33
Free snacks	32
Free coffee	30
Companywide retreats	26
Weekly free employee outings	24
On-site gym	22
Team bonding events	20

Source: Fractl survey of 2,000 U.S. workers

Better health, dental, and vision insurance topped the list, but the next most valued benefits were ones that offer flexibility and improve work-life balance. Flexible hours and work-from-home arrangements ranked highly for all respondents—benefits that typically cost employers nothing, and often save money by lowering overhead costs.

Kerry Jones is the inbound marketing manager at Fractl, where she specializes in content marketing featuring their proprietary research.

Adapted from "The Most Desirable Employee Benefits" on hbr.org, February 15, 2017 (product #HO3FSR).

team. (See the sidebar "A Fair Approach to Financial Incentives.")

The biggest problem with extrinsic rewards, by far, is that while many people believe monetary compensation is a major driver of performance, research has found little corroborating evidence. In fact, bonuses and other financial incentives in some cases can do more harm than good. "When it comes to producing lasting change in attitudes and behavior," writes Kohn, "rewards, like punishment, are strikingly ineffective. Once the rewards run out, people revert to their old behaviors." Extrinsic motivators don't change the attitudes that underlie behavior.

Unless you are a senior executive, you may not have much control over the financial and extrinsic rewards you can offer, but you do have the opportunity to provide intangible incentives that might mean more to your employees.

Intrinsic Rewards

The opposite of extrinsic incentives, intrinsic rewards produce nonquantifiable personal satisfaction, such as a sense of accomplishment, personal control over one's

A FAIR APPROACH TO FINANCIAL INCENTIVES

In theory, it's easy to dole out cash when someone performs well. But in reality, it's not that simple.

Extrinsic rewards are quantifiable, but motivation is not. How much money does it take to alter someone's behavior? Offer $100 to your sales reps if they hit their quotas, and they won't bat an eye. Offer $1 million, and you'll have their full attention, but that's not a realistic figure. No one can say for certain what the right number is—and the right number for one person may be the wrong one for someone else.

What's more, it's rarely possible to sort out individual contributions to a project or determine what they're worth. Who should be rewarded when a new car is launched, for example? Should it be the designers, the engineers, the marketing team, or the executive who oversaw the whole project? Even if it were possible to pinpoint the measure of any individual's

work, and a feeling that efforts are appreciated. Examples include intellectual stimulation, skill development, autonomy, or challenge. When intrinsically motivated, people do things for their own sense of achievement because they inherently want to.

Intrinsic rewards must be thoughtfully tailored to individuals. A meaningful reward to one employee may not move another. A conscientious contributor might be thrilled to be given the opportunity to attend a conference in their area of interest, while an ambitious rising

contribution, this form of financial reward can actually undermine both teamwork and performance.

Most employees' main concern about pay-related issues is fairness, so if you do want to use financial incentives, make them fair and consistent. Concerns about fairness should not arise when the criteria of rewards are standard, based on clear metrics, and obvious to all—especially when individual contributors are the ones being rewarded.

But the issue of fairness is harder to resolve when rewarding members of a team. "Everyone on the team should participate in the reward payout," suggest Jeremy Hope and Steve Player in *Beyond Performance Management*. Since it's nearly impossible to determine and quantify the exact contribution of a team's individual members, don't try.

star might prefer being offered face time with the CEO or an appointment to a high-level project team.

There are a variety of ways that one can encourage good work through intrinsic rewards. Here are three tactics you can incorporate into your daily routine.

Acknowledge Good Work

Recognition is one of the most powerful tools in a manager's toolbox—and a far more powerful motivator than money. "Recognition is about feeling special," explains author and motivation expert Bob Nelson, and "it is hard to feel special from a corporate program where everyone gets the same thing, like a five-year pin."[1]

When deciding how to recognize individuals, take their personalities into account. An extrovert may get a kick out of a public display, but a more introverted person might cringe at such a spectacle. Tailor your approach to what you know of their preferences—and if you aren't sure, ask. The motivation employees derive from well-tailored recognition can be significant. In his *Harvard Business Review* article, "What Great Managers Do," Marcus Buckingham describes the example of Jim Kawashima, a Walgreens manager. Jim realized that his customer service representative, Manjit, was highly competitive and measurement focused—and she thrived on public recognition. So Jim covered his office walls with charts and figures highlighting employee successes in red. Because Manjit loved to win and see her successes acknowledged, she was driven to achieve the highest sales numbers on the team. Her success galvanized the rest of the staff, and after a few months their location was ranked first out of 4,000 in a companywide selling program.

Like feedback, recognition is best delivered frequently—at least once every other week. That may seem like a lot, but if your team gathers for weekly meetings, reserving a moment every other week to acknowledge an employee's contributions will take very little time and have a big impact.

Provide Decision-Making Discretion

Employees are energized when they're empowered to make decisions that affect their own work. "Showing trust, granting autonomy, and recognizing the value of individual contributions all build employees' sense of ownership of their work and pride in performing it," says Monique Valcour, executive and career coach, in her HBR.org article, "The Power of Dignity in the Workplace." Giving your employees control over their work as their capabilities allow and supporting their efforts to achieve meaningful goals can lead to superior performance and can also serve as rich development opportunities. (We'll explore learning and development as tools for increasing engagement in section 4.)

Granting your employees the autonomy to make decisions increases their sense of ownership and control—and boosts their motivation. For example, Home Depot grants managers decision-making discretion over their own stores' merchandise and layout, rather than insisting that each outlet operate identically. Although the practice is less efficient financially, it keeps employees feeling engaged and rewarded and can stave off burnout.

Introduce Challenge

People are often capable of handling tasks that are more complex and more demanding than their managers expect and than their job descriptions require. Tackling such challenges can reward, inspire, and motivate them. In researching her book *Rookie Smarts: Why Learning Beats Knowing in the New Game of Work*, management consultant Liz Wiseman found that satisfaction increases as the level of challenge grows.

Consider giving employees higher-stakes assignments that involve more-complex problems or a bigger set of stakeholders. This could be a matter of offering a new work assignment or expanding a current one. For example, you could enlarge an employee's training session in coding to include participants from the entire organization rather than offering it to only those who are in their specific department.

You can also invite your employees to stretch their skills and grow their expertise by giving them projects they've never done before. This tactic may not work for every employee, however. "Make sure to choose people who have core aptitude or adjacent skills, but then let them learn as they go," Wiseman explains in her HBR. org article, "An Easy Way to Make Your Employees Happier." "Their comfort zones will expand, and they'll take great pride in mastering new things." Remember, though, that the learning process can be rocky—and before someone feels comfortable with a new skill, they might feel frustrated or unsure for a while.

Finally, consider redirecting a person's existing expertise by pivoting to a new problem. Many skills are transferable from one area to another; with expertise in one field, some people can quickly pick up the nuances of a related one. For example, a scientist at a pharmaceutical company shifted her research from cellular biology—her area of expertise—to oncology. She was unsure, initially, about how to do so but after a few months reported feeling invigorated, challenged, and newly creative.

NOTE

1. Harvard Management Update, "Employee Recognition and Reward When Times Are Tough," hbr.org, February 28, 2008, hbr.org/2008/02/employee-recognition-and-rewar-1.html.

CHAPTER 5

What Maslow Got Wrong About Our Psychological Needs

by Susan Fowler

At some point in their careers, most leaders have either consciously—or, more likely, unwittingly—based (or justified) their approach to motivation on Maslow's hierarchy of needs. Maslow's idea that people are motivated by satisfying lower-level needs such as food, water, shelter, and security, before they can move on to being motivated by higher-level needs such as self-actualization,

Adapted from "What Maslow's Hierarchy Won't Tell You About Motivation" on hbr.org, November 26, 2014 (product #H012BN).

is the most well-known motivation theory in the world. There is nothing wrong with helping people satisfy what Maslow characterized as lower-level needs. Improvements in workplace conditions and safety should be applauded as the right thing to do. Seeing that people have enough food and water to meet their biological needs is the humane thing to do. Getting people off the streets into healthy environments is the decent thing to do. But the truth is, individuals can experience higher-level motivation anytime and anywhere.

Despite the popularity of Maslow's hierarchy, there is not much recent data to support it. Contemporary science—specifically Dr. Edward Deci, hundreds of self-determination theory researchers, and thousands of studies—instead points to three universal psychological needs. If you really want the advantage of this new science—rather than focusing on a pyramid of needs—you should focus on *autonomy, relatedness*, and *competence*.

Autonomy is people's need to perceive that they have choices, that what they are doing is of their own volition, and that they are the source of their own actions. The way leaders frame information and situations either promotes the likelihood that a person will perceive autonomy or undermines it. To promote autonomy:

1. Frame goals and timelines as essential information to assure a person's success, rather than as dictates or ways to hold people accountable.

2. Refrain from incentivizing people through competitions and games. Few people have learned the

skill of shifting the reason why they're competing from an external one (winning a prize or gaining status) to a higher-quality one (an opportunity to fulfill a meaningful goal).

3. Don't apply pressure to perform. Sustained peak performance is a result of people acting because they *choose* to—not because they feel they *have* to.

Relatedness is people's need to care about and be cared about by others, to feel connected to others without concerns about ulterior motives, and to feel that they are contributing to something greater than themselves. Leaders have the opportunity to help people derive meaning from their work. To deepen relatedness:

1. Validate the exploration of feelings in the workplace. Be willing to ask people how they feel about an assigned project or goal and listen to their response. All behavior may not be acceptable, but all feelings are worth exploring.

2. Take time to facilitate the development of people's values at work—then help them align those values with their goals. It is impossible to link work to values if individuals don't know what their values are.

3. Connect people's work to a noble purpose.

Competence is people's need to feel effective at meeting everyday challenges and opportunities, demonstrating skill over time, and feeling a sense of growth and flourishing. Leaders can ignite people's desire to grow and learn. To develop people's competence:

1. Make resources available for learning. What message does it send about values for learning and developing competence when training budgets are the first casualty of economic cutbacks?

2. Set learning goals—not just the traditional results-oriented and outcome goals.

3. At the end of each day, instead of asking, "What did you achieve today?" ask "What did you learn today? How did you grow today in ways that will help you and others tomorrow?"

Unlike Maslow's needs, these three basic needs are not hierarchical or sequential. They are foundational to all human beings and our ability to flourish.

The exciting message to leaders is that when the three basic psychological needs are satisfied in the workplace, people experience the day-to-day, high-quality motivation that fuels passion—and all the inherent benefits that come from actively engaged employees. To take advantage of the science requires shifting your leadership focus from "What can I give people to motivate them?" to "How can I facilitate people's satisfaction of autonomy, relatedness, and competence?"

Leaders have opportunities every day to integrate these motivational practices. For example, a leader I coach was about to launch a companywide message to announce mandatory training on green solutions compliance. Ironically, his well-intentioned message dictated people's actions—undermining people's sense of autonomy and probably guaranteeing their defiance rather than compliance. His message didn't provide a values-based rationale or ask individuals to consider how their own values might be aligned with the initiative. After reconsidering his approach, he created this message embedded with ways for people to experience autonomy, relatedness, and competence:

> *There are three ways you can share our commitment for implementing green solutions as an essential part of our corporate social responsibility initiative.*
>
> - *Join others who are passionate about reducing their carbon footprint for a fun and interactive training session on November 15* (relatedness).
> - *Read the attached manifesto and take a quick quiz to see what you learned by November 18* (competence).
> - *Send us your story about what you are doing at work to be environmentally responsible by November 14* (autonomy, competence, and relatedness).
>
> *You can choose any or all three options* (autonomy). *Let us know your preference(s) by email* (autonomy) *by October 31 or stop by our table at the all-company Halloween party* (relatedness). *If you choose to opt out of all three choices* (autonomy), *please tell us what we can do to appeal more directly to your values around corporate social responsibility* (relatedness).

Don't underestimate your people's capacity—indeed, their longing—to experience high-quality motivation at work anytime and anywhere.

———————

Susan Fowler is senior consulting partner with the Ken Blanchard Companies, and author of *Why Motivating People Doesn't Work . . . And What Does: The New Science of Leading, Energizing, and Engaging.*

CHAPTER 6

A Recipe for Disengagement on Your Team

by Ron Carucci

When I speak to large groups about leadership, one question I often ask is, "How many of you have ever received a compliment from your boss that actually offended you?" Without exception, more than two-thirds of the people in the room raise their hands. When I probe further into what people found offensive about their boss's praise, the most common responses I hear are "It wasn't sincere" and "They didn't know what they were talking about."

Adapted from "What Not to Do When You're Trying to Motivate Your Team" on hbr.org, July 16, 2018 (product #H04FSI).

When leaders look like they are just applying some "motivational technique" they read about, people see right through the superficial, obligatory effort. It looks like they are checking off the "I motivated someone today" box. As Susan David writes in the introduction to this book, motivation is not something you *do to people*. People ultimately *choose* to be motivated—to give their best, go the extra mile, or offer radical ideas. The only thing leaders can do is shape the conditions under which others do, or don't, choose to be motivated. But the final choice is *theirs*.

Unfortunately, too few managers understand this, and so there is a gap between their efforts and the results they're getting. A 10-year study of more than 200,000 employees by the O. C. Tanner Learning Group shows that 79% of employees who quit their jobs cite a lack of appreciation as a key reason, and according to Gallup's 2017 "State of the American Workplace" report, only 21% agree their performance is managed in a way that motivates them to do outstanding work. Here are three of the most offensive forms of "motivating" I've seen managers employ, and three alternative approaches I've seen work wonderfully.

Drive-by Praise

Busy managers often have to squeeze in their recognition efforts to already crowded schedules. So they'll pop their heads into people's offices on the way to other meetings and say things like, "Hey, great job this morning at the pipeline review." Or they'll send a text message saying something like, "Hey, sorry I wasn't able to catch you before I left, but just read through the updated analytics and they look great. Thanks!" On the surface, these efforts seem innocuous, perhaps even positive. But to recipients, it can feel impersonal, uninformed, and inadequate if these drive-bys are the only form of recognition the manager offers.

Making Stuff Up

During a break from an executive team meeting I was facilitating, I watched one executive say to his direct report, "Just so you know, I was telling the big boss and his team this morning what an amazing job you're doing," and then give him what appeared to be an "I've got your back" wink. The only problem is that it never happened. And from the looks of it, the employee's feigned smile— "Wow, you did that for *me*?"—suggested he didn't buy it either. Employees know when their managers are being insincere or outright lying. Whether these made-up stories are well intended or not, they erode the employee's trust in the leader.

Guilt Gratitude

It's incredibly awkward when a manager who feels guilty tries to overcompensate with effusive expressions of appreciation. Leaders who may have asked for a sacrificial effort to meet a deadline will reflexively say things like, "You have no idea how much I appreciate this. I don't know what I would have done if you hadn't gotten this to me today. I owe you!" Or even worse, if their guilt is particularly intensified, they'll do it in public, which feels especially manipulative. They'll check off their "public recognition" box—a commonly suggested technique—by saying something like, "Can we all give Jennifer a round of applause for that killer presentation she pulled together?" A more truthful acknowledgment would have been, "Can we all give Jennifer a round of applause for that killer presentation she pulled together, which I neglected to ask her for until 8 p.m. last night because I forgot about this morning's customer segmentation review?"

The common shortfall among these misapplied approaches is that they all serve the leader who's giving the praise, not the recipient. If you want to direct your good intentions into more-meaningful expressions of recognition, consider these alternatives.

Ask for the Story

Nothing affirms an employee's great work more than a leader saying, "That was amazing. Tell me how you did it." By asking for, and listening intently to, the story behind an accomplishment, you acknowledge that the contribution is an extension of its contributor and help them feel that they, *and their work*, really matter. By honoring the story behind the work, you honor the results as well as the employee who reached them. You also get a view into the person's mind: how they problem-solve, where they have doubts, what parts of the work they love, and what makes them feel proud. Those insights become invaluable later. When you make assignments, you'll know what will be most gratifying for that person.

Contextualize Gratitude

Employees lower in an organization often can't see how their efforts contribute to broader strategies. One survey of more than 1,000 U.S. workers by Robert Half Management Resources shows that only 47% of employees can make the connection between their daily duties and company performance. Rather than taking for granted that those you lead fully appreciate the larger context into which their efforts fit, take the time to teach them. Tell them you appreciate their efforts not just because of how you benefit but also because of how the larger organization benefits. For example, say a manager gets his team to adopt a new technology platform as part of a beta test. You might explain that this effort is contributing to a broader change management initiative across the company and that it's setting a great example for those who are resistant to the change.

Acknowledge the Cost

No substantial contribution comes without personal cost to the one making it. Whether someone sacrificed time with family, took on the emotional toil of doing something new, or bore the political risks of a highly visible project, let them know that you understand the toll it took. Most employees hide any struggle that accompanied their efforts for fear of looking weak or incompetent. Acknowledging the challenges they may have faced makes your gratitude more credible, and makes it safer for employees to be honest with you in the future when facing difficulties.

It's a leader's job to create a recognition-rich environment in which those they lead choose to give their best.
That starts by ensuring recognition genuinely serves the
needs of those you're offering it to, not your own.

––––––––––––

Ron Carucci is cofounder and managing partner at Nava-
lent, working with CEOs and executives pursuing trans-
formational change for their organizations, leaders, and
industries. He is the best-selling author of eight books,
including the recent Amazon number one *Rising to
Power*. Follow him on Twitter @RonCarucci.

CHAPTER 7

Motivating Salespeople: What Really Works

by Thomas Steenburgh and Michael Ahearne

Sales executives are always looking for ingenious ways to motivate their teams. They stage grand kickoff meetings to announce new bonus programs. They promise exotic trips to rainmakers. When business is slow, they hold sales contests. If sales targets are missed, they blame the sales compensation plan and start from square one.

The finance organization, meanwhile, views the comp plan as an expense to manage. That's not surprising: Sales force compensation represents the single largest

---

Reprinted from *Harvard Business Review*, July–August 2012 (product #R1207D).

marketing investment for most B2B companies. In aggregate, U.S. companies alone spend more than $800 billion on it each year—three times more than they spend on advertising. So naturally finance tries to ensure that comp plans have cost-control measures designed into them. Some companies offer flat commission rates so that compensation costs rise and fall with revenues. Others cap compensation once salespeople hit certain performance targets. Still others use bonuses to control spending by pinning salespeople's quotas to Wall Street revenue targets.

But a few progressive companies have been able to coax better performance from their teams by treating their sales force like a portfolio of investments that require different levels and kinds of attention. Some salespeople have greater ability and internal drive than others, and a growing body of research suggests that stars, laggards, and core performers are motivated by different facets of comp plans. Stars seem to knock down any target that stands in their way—but may stop working if a ceiling is imposed. Laggards need more guidance and prodding to make their numbers (carrots as well as sticks, in many cases). Core performers fall somewhere in the middle; they get the least attention, even though they're the group most likely to move the needle—if they're given the proper incentives.

Accounting for individual differences raises the odds that a compensation plan will stimulate the performance of all types of salespeople. In this article we will discuss how companies can do this to deliver greater returns on investment and shift their sales-performance curve upward.

Motivating Core Performers

Ironically enough, many incentive plans come close to ignoring core performers. Why does this group tend to be off the radar screen? One reason is that sales managers don't identify with them. At many companies the managers are former rainmakers, so they pay the current rainmakers an undue amount of attention. As a consequence, core performers are often passed over for promotion and neglected at annual sales meetings. But this is not in the best interest of the company. Core performers usually represent the largest part of the sales force, and companies cannot make their numbers if they're not in the game. Here are some proven strategies for keeping them there.

Multi-tier targets

A project that Mike recently worked on with a national financial services company shows that such targets help motivate core performers. At the company a major proportion of the salespeople fell into this category. In bearish months they almost always found a way to hit their targets, but in bullish months they seldom exceeded their numbers substantially. In an effort to nudge them upward, the company experimented with tiered targets.

The first-tier target was set at a point that a majority of the company's sales agents had historically attained, the second-tier target at a point reached by a smaller percentage of the sales force, and the third-tier target at a point hit only by the company's elite. All the firm's agents were divided into two groups: The first was given targets at tiers one and three, and the second group got targets at all three tiers. The hypothesis was that tiers would act as stepping stones to guide core performers up the curve.

The tiered structure indeed had a profound impact. Core performers striving to achieve triple-tier targets significantly outsold core performers given only two tiers. By contrast, multi-tier targets did not motivate stars and laggards as much: No significant differences in performance were found for those segments.

These results suggest that core performers exert more effort if given additional tiers. Stars are presumably unaffected by the extra stepping stone because they view the top tier as attainable regardless of the number of targets. And the inattentiveness that laggards show suggests that they typically aim for and are satisfied with achieving the first-tier target.

Prizes

A research project that we're both currently working on investigates how prize structures in sales contests can engage core performers. The problem with contests is that stars usually win them. Knowing this, core performers don't bump up their own efforts. You can handicap contestants on the basis of their prior performance, which alleviates the problem to a certain degree. But that creates its own problem: What's fair about core performers' and laggards' taking home the top prizes, if stars are left with lesser prizes or no prize at all?

Ideally, sales executives would design contests so that both stars and core performers would go home satisfied. This isn't easy to do, but if you keep in mind that people are hardwired to adapt to their position in a social hierarchy, it is possible. The key is to offer gifts (not cash) for the lower-level prizes that can be seen as equal, or even superior, to the top-level prizes on some dimension. Suppose a prestigious golf vacation is awarded as a top prize and a local family getaway is awarded as a lower prize. The family getaway has a lower market value than the golf vacation, but core performers can adapt to their central position on the performance curve by shifting their preferences. They can rationalize their prize by saying, "I've golfed plenty lately—what's important to me is spending time with my family." We consistently find that core performers work harder and perform better in contests of this kind than they do in contests with cash prizes. Furthermore, their increased effort does not come at the cost of decreased effort from stars or laggards.

However, this approach won't work if the gifts offered at lower performance tiers are simply lower-grade versions of those at the top tier. Core performers will never perceive 18 holes at a run-of-the-mill golf course as more desirable than 18 holes at a prestigious course. The lower-level prize must have some quality that the higher-level one does not. In this example, it was the local getaway's family appeal that allowed core performers to remain engaged in the contest.

We've also seen that core performers near the bottom of their cadre are motivated by incentives designed to improve the performance of laggards. This happens because they fear falling into the lower category. Now let's take a look at the incentives that work for the salespeople in that group.

Motivating Laggards

The low-performing group in a sales force is usually heterogeneous: It may include new hires in need of training and senior salespeople who have become complacent, as well as people who are simply less talented and motivated than their colleagues. Most laggard groups we've observed have members whose performance can improve if the right incentives are in place. The following strategies (which include both carrots and sticks) effectively motivate the "good" laggards to move up the curve.

Pace-setting bonuses

A current study of Tom's looks at the most common carrot: the bonus. This study, based on field data from a *Fortune* 500 company that sells durable office goods, separately models the behavior of stars, core performers, and laggards within a number of different compensation plans.

The study found that removing quarterly bonuses from laggards' incentives—and keeping only an annual bonus—would decrease their overall performance (as measured by the revenues they generate) by approximately 10%. The same change would decrease the overall performance of core and star salespeople by 4% and

2%, respectively. There is no downside to including quarterly bonuses. They help laggards contribute to the bottom line without detracting from the performance of other groups.

Pace-setting goals have been found to change the behavior of low performers in other domains, too; education researchers see similar patterns among students. Weaker students need periodic quizzes throughout the semester to keep them on track. In the absence of such mechanisms, they perform poorly on comprehensive exams. By contrast, strong students—like star salespeople—make an effort independently and have less need for intermittent goals.

Natural social pressure

Managers often mention that having a high-quality pipeline of new sales talent naturally puts social pressure on low-performing salespeople. This is commonly referred to as the "man on the bench" effect, because it is similar to the pressure that second-string quarterbacks, say, place on starters in football.

In a current study, we measure the impact of bench players on the performance of existing sales teams. Using advanced econometric techniques, we compare districts with and without bench players. We've observed that salespeople in districts with a bench player perform approximately 5% better than those without one. The greatest increase in performance takes place in the laggard group. In the long run the overall increase in revenue easily outweighs the additional costs associated with hiring bench players.

When a company has a disproportionate number of laggards, it's usually the result of sales managers' reluctance to face a difficult transition period. Often managers are forced to make a trade-off between retaining chronic low performers and enduring vacant sales territories. Hiring bench players can help ease this transition.

Program-induced social pressure

Programs that put social pressure on laggards should be implemented with care. Successful programs are born out of rigorous pilot testing and are sensitive to the culture of the firm. When designed well, programs heighten laggards' sense of responsibility to the team and motivate stars to help laggards out. They avoid demoralizing people.

One company we've observed puts laggards' performance under the microscope by occasionally posting sales numbers in ascending order from laggards to stars (rather than the more conventional reverse order). Another company publicly posts a sign in its sales bull pen that lists each of its salespeople in one of three categories: starters, benchwarmers, and the penalty box. While this type of public display is relatively extreme, it seems to work within this company's competitive and transparent culture. Wins are celebrated with ostentatious prizes, such as courtside seats for sporting events and leases for Porsches. Losses are taken bitterly.

Motivating Stars

Since stars represent the most efficient portion of a company's performance curve, incentive plans should favor them. Yet in many companies sales commission rates are capped and winner-take-all prize structures dominate the incentives. A primary reason is cost control, driven largely by the finance department.

But are these practices rational? The simple answer is no. Executives who impose these cost-control measures encourage the same form of irrational behavior that Colin Camerer and his colleagues discovered in their study of New York City cabdrivers.

Camerer researched whether cabdrivers worked longer hours when more people wanted a taxi ("law of supply") or quit for the day once they reached a certain number ("income targeting"). It wasn't even close: Overwhelmingly, cabdrivers quit for the day once they reached their target. By placing caps on commissions when salespeople are hot, executives encourage stars to quit selling—just as cabbies go home early on rainy days, when their hourly earnings are highest. Companies would be better off if stars worked more intensively during times of high demand.

No ceiling on commissions

A recent study by Sanjog Misra and Harikesh Nair examines the impact of capping salespeople's pay. They looked at the compensation plan of a large U.S. contact-lens manufacturer. This company stopped paying commissions once salespeople's performance reached a quota ceiling. In response, the salespeople always held sales under the ceiling. By eliminating it and making other changes to the compensation plan, the company kept its salespeople motivated and increased revenue by about 9%.

Overachievement commissions

These are higher rates that kick in after quotas are met. For example, salespeople may earn a penny on a dollar with their regular commission rate until quotas are reached, but earn two pennies on a dollar on all sales above quotas. Tom's research at the office supply company, mentioned earlier, proves the effectiveness of overachievement incentives. Removing them from a compensation plan would reduce stars' sales by approximately 17%, the research showed. An overachievement commission rate can help keep stars in the field during the fourth quarter—often the period in which customers are most ready to buy.

Multiple winners

A study of Mike's reveals that contests with multiple winners boost sales effort and performance better than contests with winner-take-all prize structures. And Noah Lim, one of his coauthors on the study, has done further work demonstrating that more (rather than fewer) prizes should be awarded as the proportion of stars increases. This finding suggests that executives should offer at least as many prizes as there are stars in a sales force. The reason is intriguing. Increasing the number of prizes in a contest increases the chances that a laggard or a core performer will win a prize in place of a star, which motivates stars to work harder.

On the whole, these results show that frugality toward top salespeople is detrimental to firm performance.

Shift Your Performance Curve Upward

Together, we have more than 40 years' experience working with companies on sales-related problems. When we first meet with executives, we always ask which decisions they sweat over the most. Deciding how to compensate salespeople is invariably at or near the top of the list. When we follow up by asking whether they have enough information to support their comp-related decisions, they nearly always say no.

It's time for that to change. We've reported here on research that reveals that salespeople at different points on the performance curve will respond to different incentives, and we hope that managers will think about the implications for their firms—and follow that stream of research as it develops. But there's no reason to rely just on studies being done by academics. We hope that companies will develop their own field experiments and learn what works best for their salespeople.

The first step for any company is to get a clear understanding of its own performance curve. Ideally, this would be done through sophisticated econometric methods, but an approximation can be obtained as follows: If you simply calculate each salesperson's performance against sales targets and then create a histogram of those data, you'll have a rough understanding of whether your company's curve is normal (mostly core performers, with about equal numbers of laggards and stars), laggard-heavy, or star-heavy. The shape of the curve will suggest which incentives will give you the most leverage. (If you have a disproportionate number of laggards, you'll want to focus first on pace-setting bonuses and natural social pressure, for example.)

But remember, the existing sales culture can't be replaced all at once. Rather than set up a whole new comp structure, you should form a hypothesis about one element of the plan—that your laggards would perform better with more-frequent pace-setting bonuses, perhaps. Design an experiment that includes both a treatment and a control group. Then pilot the change in just one part of the sales organization. Test one hypothesis at a time, in a limited pilot run. (For advice about how to do that, see "A Step-by-Step Guide to Smart Business Experiments," by Eric T. Anderson and Duncan Simester, HBR March 2011.)

Sales compensation plans that take into account the different needs of different salespeople—and that are based on real evidence rather than assumptions—will ensure that your sales department gets a significantly higher return on its investments.

Thomas Steenburgh is an associate professor of marketing at the University of Virginia's Darden School of Business. **Michael Ahearne** is the C.T. Bauer Chaired Professor in Marketing at the University of Houston and the executive director of the Sales Excellence Institute.

CHAPTER 8

One Engagement Strategy Does Not Fit All

by Natalie Baumgartner

You've probably heard these stories before: A coaching program that worked for one employee failed with another who's up against the same hurdles. A reward system that increased performance on one team actually led to disgruntled workers in another group. Talent management programs that were a raging success in one instance were replicated in another and failed.

By using the same reward systems, the same engagement tactics, the same coaching programs, you're

---

Adapted from content posted on hbr.org, November 26, 2014 (product #H012WG).

managing your employees as if they are all the same person. They're not. So stop treating them like clones.

Managing people as if they are all identical doesn't work because your people are actually strikingly different from one another. To illustrate this fact, my company RoundPegg recently conducted research that analyzed the personal values held in 763 million one-to-one relationships (for example, you to your colleague, you to your boss, and so forth) and found that only three people shared the same exact set of 18 personal values.

That means that each of your employees is not just one in a million; they are one in 250 million.

Given how differently every employee is wired, you can't take a cookie-cutter approach to talent management. Your people need to be motivated differently based on their personal wiring, something that the blind replication of talent management programs fails to take into account.

So why do intelligent, thoughtful leaders assume they can manage their talent in the same way, every time, in the first place? It all goes back to how we're wired. Nearly 70 years ago, cognitive psychologists identified a phenomenon called the false-consensus bias, which leads people to assume everyone thinks in the same way, that there is a general consensus regarding beliefs and values. That assumption of similarity can result in leaders developing or endorsing talent management programs that are a one-stop shop.

An example of what this looks like in practice comes from a major international healthcare organization we recently worked with. In an attempt to increase employee engagement on one of their struggling teams, they put in place a financial bonus system that had worked exceptionally well with another team. They assumed their success would be replicated, but it nearly spurred a revolt. The problem? Leadership wasn't aware of the striking difference in personal values between the two teams.

While the members of the team that originally benefited from this bonus system placed a great deal of personal value on receiving high pay for good performance, the other team's members placed significantly more value on receiving opportunities for professional growth. Once the team's leaders understood this, they shifted their engagement strategy to focus on providing professional development opportunities to the struggling group. They saw an almost immediate uptick in employee performance, which translated to an 11% increase in patient satisfaction. They were successful because they made it personal, keeping in mind these two important rules:

Know Your People

Start by more explicitly understanding who your employees are. Leaders at every level need to be able to accurately identify the specific values that are most important to the people who report to them. To figure out what uniquely drives them, create a list of simple values and ask your employees—via surveys, interviews or focus groups—which are the most important to them as individuals. This process will take time and energy, especially at first. It requires focus and the willingness to try something that may turn heads within your company.

However, you will quickly learn a lot about your people and about how to best support them—information that can fundamentally change their work experience.

Leverage Their Strengths

Provide accessible resources to help your people to function at their best, while also reinforcing the culture you want to grow within your company. Once you've identified the values that are important to your employees, use that information to create two or three development goals for each of them that bridge the gap between their personal values and your company's culture. For example, if one of your people values risk-taking but your organization aspires to maintain stability, give that employee the specific task of exploring and evaluating new, perhaps untested, technology that can be used to enhance internal stability, such as social networking tools.

IBM has been a pioneer in the world of personalized employee development. One approach they've used to support their people is a mentorship matching program. Rather than creating a one-size-fits-all employee development system, the company provides an online database that allows employees to find a mentorship relationship that can help them fulfill their development objectives—something like increasing their knowledge about a new area of the business, expanding a technical skill set, or crafting a new leadership strategy. Potential mentoring relationships include traditional senior-to-junior mentoring, peer mentoring, virtual group mentoring, and reverse junior-to-senior mentoring for experienced executives looking to master social media or new technologies. There are no assumptions around who should mentor whom, and mentor relationships exist across business units and geographical locations.

IBM reports that their mentoring program has resulted in an overall uptick in strategic collaboration across the company, and a more specific increase in employee skill development. It provides their people with an opportunity to get the support that matters most to them, based on who they are and what they're interested in.

It's time for all of us to make talent management this personal. Supporting, developing, and engaging people as if they are all identical is wrongheaded. Rather than assuming your people are clones, find out what makes them unique and create meaningful processes to help them be their best.

———————

Dr. Natalie Baumgartner is a cofounder and the chief psychologist at RoundPegg, a culture management software platform leveraging predictive talent analytics. She serves on the board of the Consulting Psychology Division of the American Psychological Association.

Make Work More Meaningful

CHAPTER 9

The Power of Small Wins

by Teresa Amabile and Steve Kramer

What is the best way to drive innovative work inside organizations? Important clues hide in the stories of world-renowned creators. It turns out that ordinary scientists, marketers, programmers, and other unsung knowledge workers, whose jobs require creative productivity every day, have more in common with famous innovators than most managers realize. The workday events that ignite their emotions, fuel their motivation, and trigger their perceptions are fundamentally the same.

The Double Helix, James Watson's 1968 memoir about discovering the structure of DNA, describes the

---

Reprinted from *Harvard Business Review*, May 2011 (product #R1105C).

roller coaster of emotions he and Francis Crick experienced through the progress and setbacks of the work that eventually earned them the Nobel Prize. After the excitement of their first attempt to build a DNA model, Watson and Crick noticed some serious flaws. According to Watson, "Our first minutes with the models . . . were not joyous." Later that evening, "a shape began to emerge which brought back our spirits." But when they showed their "breakthrough" to colleagues, they found that their model would not work. Dark days of doubt and ebbing motivation followed. When the duo finally had their bona fide breakthrough, and their colleagues found no fault with it, Watson wrote, "My morale skyrocketed, for I suspected that we now had the answer to the riddle." Watson and Crick were so driven by this success that they practically lived in the lab, trying to complete the work.

Throughout these episodes, Watson and Crick's progress—or lack thereof—ruled their reactions. In our recent research on creative work inside businesses, we stumbled upon a remarkably similar phenomenon. Through exhaustive analysis of diaries kept by knowledge workers, we discovered the *progress principle*: Of all the things that can boost emotions, motivation, and perceptions during a workday, the single most important is making progress in meaningful work. And the more frequently people experience that sense of progress, the more likely they are to be creatively productive in the long run. Whether they are trying to solve a major scientific mystery or simply produce a high-quality product or service, everyday progress—even a small win—can make all the difference in how they feel and perform.

The power of progress is fundamental to human nature, but few managers understand it or know how to leverage progress to boost motivation. In fact, work motivation has been a subject of long-standing debate. In a survey asking about the keys to motivating workers, we found that some managers ranked recognition for good work as most important, while others put more stock in tangible incentives. Some focused on the value of interpersonal support, while still others thought clear goals were the answer. Interestingly, very few of our surveyed managers ranked progress first.

If you are a manager, the progress principle holds clear implications for where to focus your efforts. It suggests that you have more influence than you may realize over employees' well-being, motivation, and creative output. Knowing what serves to catalyze and nourish progress—and what does the opposite—turns out to be the key to effectively managing people and their work.

In this article, we share what we have learned about the power of progress and how managers can leverage it. We spell out how a focus on progress translates into concrete managerial actions and provide a checklist to help make such behaviors habitual. But to clarify why those actions are so potent, we first describe our research and what the knowledge workers' diaries revealed about their *inner work lives*.

Inner Work Life and Performance

For nearly 15 years, we have been studying the psychological experiences and the performance of people doing complex work inside organizations. Early on, we realized that a central driver of creative, productive performance was the quality of a person's inner work life—the mix of emotions, motivations, and perceptions over the course of a workday. How happy workers feel; how motivated they are by an intrinsic interest in the work; how positively they view their organization, their management, their team, their work, and themselves—all these combine either to push them to higher levels of achievement or to drag them down.

To understand such interior dynamics better, we asked members of project teams to respond individually to an end-of-day e-mail survey during the course of the project—just over four months, on average. (For more on this research, see our article "Inner Work Life: Understanding the Subtext of Business Performance," HBR May 2007.) The projects—inventing kitchen gadgets, managing product lines of cleaning tools, and solving complex IT problems for a hotel empire, for example—all involved creativity. The daily survey inquired about participants' emotions and moods, motivation levels, and perceptions of the work environment that day, as well as what work they did and what events stood out in their minds.

Twenty-six project teams from seven companies participated, comprising 238 individuals. This yielded nearly 12,000 diary entries. Naturally, every individual in our population experienced ups and downs. Our goal was to discover the states of inner work life and the workday events that correlated with the highest levels of creative output.

In a dramatic rebuttal to the commonplace claim that high pressure and fear spur achievement, we found that, at least in the realm of knowledge work, people are more creative and productive when their inner work lives are positive—when they feel happy, are intrinsically motivated by the work itself, and have positive perceptions of their colleagues and the organization. Moreover, in those positive states, people are more committed to the work and more collegial toward those around them. Inner work life, we saw, can fluctuate from one day to the next—sometimes wildly—and performance along with it. A person's inner work life on a given day fuels his or her performance for the day and can even affect performance the *next* day.

Once this *inner work life effect* became clear, our inquiry turned to whether and how managerial action could set it in motion. What events could evoke positive or negative emotions, motivations, and perceptions? The answers were tucked within our research participants' diary entries. There are predictable triggers that inflate or deflate inner work life, and, even accounting for variation among individuals, they are pretty much the same for everyone.

The Power of Progress

Our hunt for inner work life triggers led us to the progress principle. When we compared our research participants' best and worst days (based on their overall mood, specific emotions, and motivation levels), we found that the most common event triggering a "best day" was any progress in the work by the individual or the team. The most common event triggering a "worst day" was a setback.

Consider, for example, how progress relates to one component of inner work life: overall mood ratings. Steps forward occurred on 76% of people's best-mood days. By contrast, setbacks occurred on only 13% of those days. (See figure 9-1.)

Two other types of inner work life triggers also occur frequently on best days: *Catalysts*, actions that directly support work, including help from a person or group, and *nourishers*, events such as shows of respect

FIGURE 9-1

What happens on a good day?

Progress—even a small step forward—occurs on many of the days people report being in a good mood.

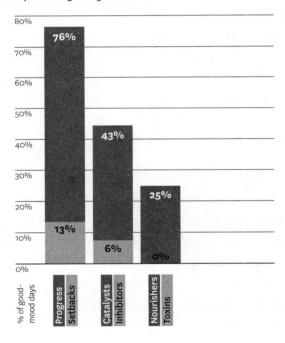

and words of encouragement. Each has an opposite: *Inhibitors*, actions that fail to support or actively hinder work, and *toxins*, discouraging or undermining events. Whereas catalysts and inhibitors are directed at the project, nourishers and toxins are directed at the person. Like setbacks, inhibitors and toxins are rare on days of great inner work life.

Events on worst-mood days are nearly the mirror image of those on best-mood days (see figure 9-2). Here,

FIGURE 9-2

What happens on a bad day?

Events on bad days—setbacks and other hindrances—are nearly the mirror image of those on good days.

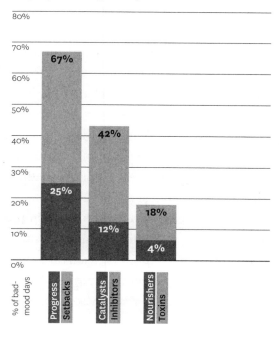

setbacks predominated, occurring on 67% of those days; progress occurred on only 25% of them. Inhibitors and toxins also marked many worst-mood days, and catalysts and nourishers were rare.

This is the progress principle made visible: If a person is motivated and happy at the end of the workday, it's a good bet that he or she made some progress. If the person drags out of the office disengaged and joyless, a setback is most likely to blame.

When we analyzed all 12,000 daily surveys filled out by our participants, we discovered that progress and setbacks influence all three aspects of inner work life. On days when they made progress, our participants reported more positive *emotions*. They not only were in a more upbeat mood in general but also expressed more joy, warmth, and pride. When they suffered setbacks, they experienced more frustration, fear, and sadness.

Motivations were also affected: On progress days, people were more intrinsically motivated—by interest in and enjoyment of the work itself. On setback days, they were not only less intrinsically motivated but also less extrinsically motivated by recognition. Apparently, setbacks can lead a person to feel generally apathetic and disinclined to do the work at all.

Perceptions differed in many ways, too. On progress days, people perceived significantly more positive challenge in their work. They saw their teams as more mutually supportive and reported more positive interactions between the teams and their supervisors. On a number of dimensions, perceptions suffered when people encountered setbacks. They found less positive challenge in the work, felt that they had less freedom in carrying it out, and reported that they had insufficient resources. On setback days, participants perceived both their teams and their supervisors as less supportive.

To be sure, our analyses establish correlations but do not prove causality. Were these changes in inner work life the result of progress and setbacks, or was the effect the other way around? The numbers alone cannot answer that. However, we do know, from reading thousands of diary entries, that more-positive perceptions, a sense of accomplishment, satisfaction, happiness, and even elation often followed progress. Here's a typical post-progress entry, from a programmer: "I smashed that bug that's been frustrating me for almost a calendar week. That may not be an event to you, but I live a very drab life, so I'm all hyped."

Likewise, we saw that deteriorating perceptions, frustration, sadness, and even disgust often followed setbacks. As another participant, a product marketer, wrote, "We spent a lot of time updating the Cost Reduction project list, and after tallying all the numbers, we are still coming up short of our goal. It is discouraging to not be able to hit it after all the time spent and hard work."

Almost certainly, the causality goes both ways, and managers can use this feedback loop between progress and inner work life to support both.

Minor Milestones

When we think about progress, we often imagine how good it feels to achieve a long-term goal or experience a major breakthrough. These big wins are great—but they are relatively rare. The good news is that even small wins can boost inner work life tremendously. Many of the progress events our research participants reported represented only minor steps forward. Yet they often evoked outsize positive reactions. Consider this diary entry from a programmer in a high-tech company, which was accompanied by very positive self-ratings of her emotions, motivations, and perceptions that day: "I figured out why something was not working correctly. I felt relieved and happy because this was a minor milestone for me."

Even ordinary, incremental progress can increase people's engagement in the work and their happiness during the workday. Across all types of events our participants reported, a notable proportion (28%) of incidents that had a minor impact on the project had a major impact on people's feelings about it. Because inner work life has such a potent effect on creativity and productivity, and because small but consistent steps forward, shared by many people, can accumulate into excellent execution, progress events that often go unnoticed are critical to the overall performance of organizations.

Unfortunately, there is a flip side. Small losses or setbacks can have an extremely negative effect on inner work life. In fact, our study and research by others show that negative events can have a more powerful impact than positive ones. Consequently, it is especially important for managers to minimize daily hassles.

Progress in Meaningful Work

We've shown how gratifying it is for workers when they are able to chip away at a goal, but recall what we said earlier: The key to motivating performance is supporting progress in *meaningful* work. Making headway boosts your inner work life, but only if the work matters to you.

Think of the most boring job you've ever had. Many people nominate their first job as a teenager—washing pots and pans in a restaurant kitchen, for example, or checking coats at a museum. In jobs like those, the power of progress seems elusive. No matter how hard you work, there are always more pots to wash and coats to check; only punching the time clock at the end of the day or getting the paycheck at the end of the week yields a sense of accomplishment.

In jobs with much more challenge and room for creativity, like the ones our research participants had, simply "making progress"—getting tasks done—doesn't guarantee a good inner work life, either. You may have experienced this rude fact in your own job, on days (or in projects) when you felt demotivated, devalued, and frustrated, even though you worked hard and got things done. The likely cause is your perception of the completed tasks as peripheral or irrelevant. For the progress principle to operate, the work must be meaningful to the person doing it.

In 1983, Steve Jobs was trying to entice John Sculley to leave a wildly successful career at PepsiCo to become

Apple's new CEO. Jobs reportedly asked him, "Do you want to spend the rest of your life selling sugared water or do you want a chance to change the world?" In making his pitch, Jobs leveraged a potent psychological force: the deep-seated human desire to do meaningful work.

Fortunately, to feel meaningful, work doesn't have to involve putting the first personal computers in the hands of ordinary people, or alleviating poverty, or helping to cure cancer. Work with less profound importance to society can matter if it contributes value to something or someone important to the worker. Meaning can be as simple as making a useful and high-quality product for a customer or providing a genuine service for a community. It can be supporting a colleague or boosting an organization's profits by reducing inefficiencies in a production process. Whether the goals are lofty or modest, as long as they are meaningful to the worker and it is clear how his or her efforts contribute to them, progress toward them can galvanize inner work life.

In principle, managers shouldn't have to go to extraordinary lengths to infuse jobs with meaning. Most jobs in modern organizations are potentially meaningful for the people doing them. However, managers can make sure that employees know just how their work is contributing. And, most important, they can avoid actions that negate its value. (See the sidebar "How Work Gets Stripped of Its Meaning.") All the participants in our research were doing work that should have been meaningful; no one was washing pots or checking coats. Shockingly often, however, we saw potentially important, challenging work losing its power to inspire.

HOW WORK GETS STRIPPED OF ITS MEANING

Diary entries from 238 knowledge workers who were members of creative project teams revealed four primary ways in which managers unwittingly drain work of its meaning.

One

Managers may dismiss the importance of employees' work or ideas. Consider the case of Richard, a senior lab technician at a chemical company, who found meaning in helping his new-product development team solve complex technical problems. However, in team meetings over the course of a three-week period, Richard perceived that his team leader was ignoring his suggestions and those of his teammates. As a result, he felt that his contributions were not meaningful, and his spirits flagged. When at last he believed that he was again making a substantive contribution to the success of the project, his mood improved dramatically: *I felt much better at today's team meeting. I felt that my opinions and information were important to the project and that we have made some progress.*

Two

They may destroy employees' sense of ownership of their work. Frequent and abrupt reassignments often have this effect. This happened repeatedly to the members of a product development team in a giant

(continued)

> ### HOW WORK GETS STRIPPED OF ITS MEANING
>
> consumer products company, as described by team member Bruce: *As I've been handing over some projects, I do realize that I don't like to give them up. Especially when you have been with them from the start and are nearly to the end. You lose ownership. This happens to us way too often.*
>
> **Three**
>
> Managers may send the message that the work employees are doing will never see the light of day. They can signal this—unintentionally—by shifting their priorities or changing their minds about how something should be done. We saw the latter in an internet technology company after user-interface developer Burt had spent weeks designing seamless transitions for non-English-speaking users. Not surprisingly, Burt's mood was seriously marred on the day he reported

Supporting Progress: Catalysts and Nourishers

What can managers do to ensure that people are motivated, committed, and happy? How can they support workers' daily progress? They can use catalysts and nourishers, the other kinds of frequent "best day" events we discovered.

Catalysts are actions that support work. They include setting clear goals, allowing autonomy, providing suffi-

this incident: *Other options for the international [interfaces] were [given] to the team during a team meeting, which could render the work I am doing useless.*

Four

They may neglect to inform employees about unexpected changes in a customer's priorities. Often, this arises from poor customer management or inadequate communication within the company. For example, Stuart, a data transformation expert at an IT company, reported deep frustration and low motivation on the day he learned that weeks of the team's hard work might have been for naught: *Found out that there is a strong possibility that the project may not be going forward, due to a shift in the client's agenda. Therefore, there is a strong possibility that all the time and effort put into the project was a waste of our time.*

cient resources and time, helping with the work, openly learning from problems and successes, and allowing a free exchange of ideas. Their opposites, inhibitors, include failing to provide support and actively interfering with the work. Because of their impact on progress, catalysts and inhibitors ultimately affect inner work life. But they also have a more immediate impact: When people realize that they have clear and meaningful goals, sufficient resources, helpful colleagues, and so on, they get an instant boost to their emotions, their motivation to do a great job, and their perceptions of the work and the organization.

Nourishers are acts of interpersonal support, such as respect and recognition, encouragement, emotional comfort, and opportunities for affiliation. Toxins, their opposites, include disrespect, discouragement, disregard for emotions, and interpersonal conflict. For good and for ill, nourishers and toxins affect inner work life directly and immediately.

Catalysts and nourishers—and their opposites—can alter the meaningfulness of work by shifting people's perceptions of their jobs and even themselves. For instance, when a manager makes sure that people have the resources they need, it signals to them that what they are doing is important and valuable. When managers recognize people for the work they do, it signals that they are important to the organization. In this way, catalysts and nourishers can lend greater meaning to the work—and amplify the operation of the progress principle.

The managerial actions that constitute catalysts and nourishers are not particularly mysterious; they may sound like Management 101, if not just common sense and common decency. But our diary study reminded us how often they are ignored or forgotten. Even some of the more attentive managers in the companies we studied did not consistently provide catalysts and nourishers. For example, a supply-chain specialist named Michael was, in many ways and on most days, an excellent subteam manager. But he was occasionally so overwhelmed that he became toxic toward his people. When a supplier failed to complete a "hot" order on time and Michael's team had to resort to air shipping to meet the customer's deadline, he realized that the profit margin on the sale would be blown. In irritation, he lashed out at his subordinates, demeaning the solid work they had done and disregarding their own frustration with the supplier. In his diary, he admitted as much: *As of Friday, we have spent $28,000 in air freight to send 1,500 $30 spray jet mops to our number two customer. Another 2,800 remain on this order, and there is a good probability that they too will gain wings. I have turned from the kindly Supply Chain Manager into the black-masked executioner. All similarity to civility is gone, our backs are against the wall, flight is not possible, therefore fight is probable.*

Even when managers don't have their backs against the wall, developing long-term strategy and launching new initiatives can often seem more important—and perhaps sexier—than making sure that subordinates have what they need to make steady progress and feel supported as human beings. But as we saw repeatedly in our research, even the best strategy will fail if managers ignore the people working in the trenches to execute it.

A Model Manager—and a Tool for Emulating Him

We could explain the many (and largely unsurprising) moves that can catalyze progress and nourish spirits, but it may be more useful to give an example of a manager who consistently used those moves—and then to provide a simple tool that can help any manager do so.

95

Our model manager is Graham, whom we observed leading a small team of chemical engineers within a multinational European firm we'll call Kruger-Bern. The mission of the team's NewPoly project was clear and meaningful enough: develop a safe, biodegradable polymer to replace petrochemicals in cosmetics and, eventually, in a wide range of consumer products. As in many large firms, however, the project was nested in a confusing and sometimes threatening corporate setting of shifting top-management priorities, conflicting signals, and wavering commitments. Resources were uncomfortably tight, and uncertainty loomed over the project's future—and every team member's career. Even worse, an incident early in the project, in which an important customer reacted angrily to a sample, left the team reeling. Yet Graham was able to sustain team members' inner work lives by repeatedly and visibly removing obstacles, materially supporting progress, and emotionally supporting the team.

Graham's management approach excelled in four ways. First, he established a positive climate, one event at a time, which set behavioral norms for the entire team. When the customer complaint stopped the project in its tracks, for example, he engaged immediately with the team to analyze the problem, without recriminations, and develop a plan for repairing the relationship. In doing so, he modeled how to respond to crises in the work: not by panicking or pointing fingers but by identifying problems and their causes, and developing a coordinated action plan. This is both a practical approach and a great way to give subordinates a sense of forward movement even in the face of the missteps and failures inherent in any complex project.

Second, Graham stayed attuned to his team's everyday activities and progress. In fact, the nonjudgmental climate he had established made this happen naturally. Team members updated him frequently—without being asked—on their setbacks, progress, and plans. At one point, one of his hardest-working colleagues, Brady, had to abort a trial of a new material because he couldn't get the parameters right on the equipment. It was bad news, because the NewPoly team had access to the equipment only one day a week, but Brady immediately informed Graham. In his diary entry that evening, Brady noted, "He didn't like the lost week but seemed to understand." That understanding assured Graham's place in the stream of information that would allow him to give his people just what they needed to make progress.

Third, Graham targeted his support according to recent events in the team and the project. Each day, he could anticipate what type of intervention—a catalyst or the removal of an inhibitor; a nourisher or some antidote to a toxin—would have the most impact on team members' inner work lives and progress. And if he could not make that judgment, he asked. Most days it was not hard to figure out, as on the day he received some uplifting news about his bosses' commitment to the project. He knew the team was jittery about a rumored corporate reorganization and could use the encouragement. Even though the clarification came during a well-earned vacation day, he immediately got on the phone to relay the good news to the team.

Finally, Graham established himself as a resource for team members, rather than a micromanager; he was sure to *check in* while never seeming to *check up* on them. Superficially, checking in and checking up seem quite similar, but micromanagers make four kinds of mistakes. First, they fail to allow autonomy in carrying out the work. Unlike Graham, who gave the NewPoly team a clear strategic goal but respected members' ideas about how to meet it, micromanagers dictate every move. Second, they frequently ask subordinates about their work without providing any real help. By contrast, when one of Graham's team members reported problems, Graham helped analyze them—remaining open to alternative interpretations—and often ended up helping to get things back on track. Third, micromanagers are quick to affix personal blame when problems arise, leading subordinates to hide problems rather than honestly discuss how to surmount them, as Graham did with Brady. And fourth, micromanagers tend to hoard information to use as a secret weapon. Few realize how damaging this is to inner work life. When subordinates perceive that a manager is withholding potentially useful information, they feel infantilized, their motivation wanes, and their work is handicapped. Graham was quick to communicate upper management's views of the project, customers' opinions and needs, and possible sources of assistance or resistance within and outside the organization.

In all those ways, Graham sustained his team's positive emotions, intrinsic motivation, and favorable perceptions. His actions serve as a powerful example of how managers at any level can approach each day determined to foster progress.

We know that many managers, however well-intentioned, will find it hard to establish the habits that seemed to come so naturally to Graham. Awareness, of course, is the first step. However, turning an awareness of the importance of inner work life into routine action takes discipline. With that in mind, we developed a checklist for managers to consult on a daily basis (see figure 9-3). The aim of the checklist is managing for meaningful progress, one day at a time.

The Progress Loop

Inner work life drives performance; in turn, good performance, which depends on consistent progress, enhances inner work life. We call this the *progress loop*; it reveals the potential for self-reinforcing benefits.

So, the most important implication of the progress principle is this: By supporting people and their daily progress in meaningful work, managers improve not only the inner work lives of their employees but also the organization's long-term performance, which enhances inner work life even more. Of course, there is a dark side—the possibility of negative feedback loops. If managers fail to support progress and the people trying to make it, inner work life suffers and so does performance; and degraded performance further undermines inner work life.

A second implication of the progress principle is that managers needn't fret about trying to read the psyches of their workers, or manipulate complicated incentive schemes, to ensure that employees are motivated and happy. As long as they show basic respect and consideration, they can focus on supporting the work itself.

99

FIGURE 9-3

The daily progress checklist

Near the end of each workday, use this checklist to review the day and plan your managerial actions for the next day. After a few days, you will be able to identify issues by scanning the boldface words. First, focus on progress and setbacks and think about specific events (catalysts, nourishers, inhibitors, and toxins) that contributed to them. Next, consider any clear inner-work-life clues and what further information they provide about progress and other events. Finally, prioritize for action. The action plan for the next day is the most important part of your daily review: What is the one thing you can do to best facilitate progress?

Progress

Which 1 or 2 events today indicated either a small win or a possible breakthrough? (Describe briefly.)

_____

_____

_____

Catalysts

☐ Did the team have clear short- and long-term **goals** for meaningful work?

☐ Did team members have sufficient **autonomy** to solve problems and take ownership of the project?

☐ Did they have all the **resources** they needed to move forward efficiently?

☐ Did they have sufficient **time** to focus on meaningful work?

☐ Did I give or get them **help** when they needed or requested it? Did I encourage team members to help one another?

☐ Did I discuss **lessons** from today's successes and problems with my team?

☐ Did I help **ideas** flow freely within the group?

Nourishers

☐ Did I show **respect** to team members by recognizing their contributions to progress, attending to their ideas, and treating them as trusted professionals?

☐ Did I **encourage** team members who faced difficult challenges?

☐ Did I **support** team members who had a personal or professional problem?

☐ Is there a sense of personal and professional **affiliation** and camaraderie within the team?

Setbacks

Which 1 or 2 events today indicated either a small setback
or a possible crisis? (Describe briefly.)

_____
_____
_____

Inhibitors

☐ Was there any confusion
regarding long- or short-term
goals for meaningful work?

☐ Were team members overly
constrained in their ability
to solve problems and feel
ownership of the project?

☐ Did they lack any of the
resources they needed to
move forward effectively?

☐ Did they lack sufficient **time** to
focus on meaningful work?

☐ Did I or others fail to provide
needed or requested **help**?

☐ Did I "punish" failure or
neglect to find **lessons** and/or
opportunities in problems and
successes?

☐ Did I or others cut off the
presentation or debate of
ideas prematurely?

Toxins

☐ Did I **disrespect** any team
members by failing to
recognize their contributions
to progress, not attending to
their ideas, or not treating
them as trusted professionals?

☐ Did I **discourage** a member of
the team in any way?

☐ Did I **neglect** a team member
who had a personal or
professional problem?

☐ Is there tension or
antagonism among members
of the team or between team
members and me?

Inner work life

Did I see any indications of the quality of my subordinates' inner work
lives today? _____

Perceptions of the work, team, management, firm _____

Emotions _____

Motivation _____

What specific events might have affected inner work life today? _____

_____

(continued)

FIGURE 9-3

The daily progress checklist (*continued*)

Action plan

What can I do tomorrow to strengthen the catalysts and
nourishers identified and provide the ones that are lacking?

_____

_____

_____

What can I do tomorrow to start eliminating the inhibitors
and toxins identified?

_____

_____

_____

To become an effective manager, you must learn to set
this positive feedback loop in motion. That may require
a significant shift. Business schools, business books, and
managers themselves usually focus on managing organizations or people. But if you focus on managing progress,
the management of people—and even of entire organizations—becomes much more feasible. You won't have to
figure out how to x-ray the inner work lives of subordinates; if you facilitate their steady progress in meaningful
work, make that progress salient to them, and treat them
well, they will experience the emotions, motivations, and
perceptions necessary for great performance. Their superior work will contribute to organizational success. And
here's the beauty of it: They will love their jobs.

———————

Teresa Amabile is Edsel Bryant Ford Professor of Business Administration at Harvard Business School. She
researches what makes people creative, productive,

happy, and motivated at work. The author of two books and over 100 scholarly papers, she holds a doctorate in psychology from Stanford University. **Steven J. Kramer** is an independent researcher, writer, and consultant in Wayland, Massachusetts. He is a coauthor of "Creativity Under the Gun" (HBR August 2002) and "Inner Work Life" (HBR May 2007). They are the authors of *The Progress Principle: Using Small Wins to Ignite Joy, Engagement, and Creativity at Work* (Harvard Business Review Press, 2011).

CHAPTER 10

The Best Leaders Show People That Their Work Matters

**by Lewis Garrad and
Tomas Chamorro-Premuzic**

There is a widely shared story about a cleaner at NASA who, when asked by JFK what his job was, responded, "I'm helping to put a man on the moon." This anecdote is often used to show how even the most mundane job can be seen as meaningful with the right mindset and under a good leadership.

Today, more and more employees demand much more than a good salary from their jobs. Money may lure

Adapted from "How to Make Work More Meaningful for Your Team" on hbr.org, August 9, 2017 (product #H03U4D).

people into jobs, but purpose, meaning, and the prospect of interesting and valuable work determine both their tenure and how hard they will work while they are on the job. Finding meaning at work has become so important that there are even public rankings for the most meaningful jobs. Although there are many factors determining how appealing jobs tend to be, those that contribute to improving other people's lives (such as healthcare and social work) are ranked at the top. Interestingly, meta-analytic studies indicate that there is only a marginal association between pay and job satisfaction. A lawyer who earns $150,000 a year is no more engaged than a freelance designer who earns $35,000 a year.

Research consistently shows that people experiencing meaningful work report better health, well-being, teamwork, and engagement; they bounce back faster from setbacks and are more likely to view mistakes as learning opportunities rather than failures. In other words, people at work are more likely to thrive and grow when they experience their job as meaningful. This is why businesses with a stronger and clearer sense of purpose tend to have better financial performance. Unsurprisingly, the most successful companies in the world are also the best places to work.

Over the past few decades, a great deal of research has shown that leaders play a significant part in helping employees understand why their roles matter. Furthermore, the leadership characteristics that enable these cultures of meaning and purpose to engage employees are a reflection of a leader's personality—which has been proven to have a strong impact on team and organizational performance.

In particular, research suggests that there are four key personality characteristics that determine leaders' ability to make other people's jobs more meaningful, namely:

They are curious and inquisitive

Studies show that people tend to experience work as meaningful when they feel like they are contributing to creating something new—especially when they feel able to explore, connect, and have an impact. Curious leaders help people find meaning at work by exploring, asking questions, and engaging people in ideas about the future. In a way, curious leaders help employees find something meaningful by providing a wider range of possibilities for how work gets done, as opposed to being very prescriptive and micromanaging people. Curious leaders are also more likely to get bored and detest monotony, so they will always be looking for people to come up with new ideas to make their own experience of work more interesting.

They are challenging and relentless

One of the greatest problems organizations must solve is the inertia and stagnation that follow success, or even its anticipation. Research by Heather Barry Kappes and Gabriele Oettingen shows that optimistic people who expect to do well don't try as hard as people who expect to struggle or fail.[1] Leaders who remain ambitious in the face of both failure and success, and who push their people to remain dissatisfied with their accomplishments, instill a deeper sense of purpose in their teams and organizations. As a result employees feel a sense of progress, reinvention, and growth, which in turn results in a more meaningful and positive work experience.

They hire for values and culture fit

Research shows that people find something valuable only if it aligns with their core needs and motives. This is why the fit between an individual's personal values and the culture of the organization they work in is such an important driver of their performance. In fact, you are better off not hiring the best, but instead people who are a good fit for your organization. Values function like an inner compass or lens through which we assign meaning to the world. Leaders who pay attention to what *each* individual values are more likely to hire people who will find it easier to connect with their colleagues and the wider organization, all of which help to drive a sense of meaning.

They are able to trust people

Most people hate being micromanaged. Overpowering and controlling bosses are a serious source of disempowerment for employees. This drains the impact from the work they do and makes them feel worthless. In stark contrast, leaders who know how to trust people are more likely to give them room to experiment and grow. In particular, they help people mold their roles—something researchers call job crafting (a topic we'll discuss in more detail in chapter 16). Employees who customize their job tend to feel a much greater sense of importance and value because they feel that their manager actually trusts them.

Note that all the above four qualities ought to exist in concert. A boss who is relentless but not trusting might seek to "keep people on their toes" by being erratic or unpredictable—a sure way to hurt performance and morale. A boss who is challenging but not curious may come across as a bully, while a boss who's trusting but not challenging will seem like a pushover. In short, there is a clear difference between making work meaningful and making it fun or easy, just like there is a big difference between an engaged and a happy employee. Whereas engagement results in enthusiasm, drive, and motivation—all of which increase performance and are therefore valuable to the organization—happiness can lead to complacency. To be a good leader, focus on helping employees find meaning in their achievements, rather than just enjoy their time at the office.

Lewis Garrad, a chartered organizational psychologist, is the growth markets lead for Mercer | Sirota, an employee research specialist. He is focused on the design and deployment of employee attitude research programs, talent assessment, and performance interventions. Follow him on Twitter @lewisgarrad. **Tomas Chamorro-Premuzic** is the chief talent scientist at ManpowerGroup, a professor of business psychology at University College London and at Columbia University, and an associate at Harvard's Entrepreneurial Finance Lab. He's the author of *Why Do So Many Incompetent Men Become Leaders? (And How to Fix It)* (Harvard Business Review Press, 2019). Follow him on Twitter @drtcp or at www .drtomascp.com.

NOTE

1. Heather Barry Kappes and Gabriele Oettingen, "Positive Fantasies about Idealized Futures Sap Energy," *Journal of Experimental Psychology* 47 (2011): 719–729.

CHAPTER 11

Great Storytelling Connects Employees to Their Work

by Joseph Grenny

I once spent a few delicious days studying Union Square Hospitality Group (USHG), a collection of high-end, casual eateries started by the famed New York restaurateur, Danny Meyer. He had recently claimed the key to his success was creating a "culture of hospitality." I set out to discover how.

One day, at his Shake Shack (now a juggernaut global chain) in Madison Square Park, an employee I'll call Bert

Adapted from content posted on hbr.org, September 25, 2017 (product #H03WIH).

was dragging a bit. Bert was relatively new and hadn't really bought into the whole *hospitality* thing. He was sneaking peeks at his cell phone while pretending to be busy around the outdoor dining area when his supervisor spotted him and torpedoed toward him.

Most organizations have a few Berts in them. In fact, let's be honest. Most of us are somewhat like Bert much of the time. We go through the motions, phoning it in. Measures of discretionary effort—the gap between what we're giving and what we're capable of giving—show that most of us are *checked out* more often than *all in*. The consequence is not just lower productivity; it is lower quality of life. Half-hearted effort isn't fun.

Fortunately, there is a lot a leader can do to help employees feel a deeper sense of motivation (and resultant satisfaction) in their work. And the first place to begin is with connection.

Connection happens when you see past the details of a task to its human consequences. When you feel connected to the moral purpose of your work, you behave differently. Now "moral purpose" might sound lofty but it needn't mean saving a puppy or curing cancer; it can involve any kind of human service. And at the end of the day, all business is about service.

That's where leaders come in. The first responsibility of leaders—whether frontline supervisors, middle managers, or executives—is to compensate for the inevitable alienation that complex organizations create, and provide employees with a visceral connection to the human purpose they serve. And that's what I observed Danny Meyer's leaders doing better than most.

What would you guess the Shake Shack supervisor did with Bert? Deliver a reprimand? ("Pick up the pace, Bert!") Lay on a guilt trip? ("The rest of the team is picking up your slack!") Discipline? ("I'm putting you on notice!") The supervisor did none of these. Instead, *she told a story.*

As Bert scrutinized his phone he stood next to spattered and cluttered dining tables. Guests passed him on their way to order food. The supervisor pulled up in front of him, put her hand on his shoulder, and said in a serious and sincere tone, "Hey Bert, twenty minutes ago a young mother left her two-year-old daughter on one of these chairs while she went to the order window to buy their food. When she walked away, her daughter began sweeping her hand back and forth over the table that was smeared with ketchup from one of our previous guests. Then she began licking it off her hand." Bert cringed. Panicked, he looked at the tables to see which ones might put the next two-year-old at risk of ketchup-borne disease and began wiping them down.

Leaders can maintain a lively sense of connection, as the Shake Shack manager did, through storytelling. It needn't be an elaborate ritual involving an audience gathered for a relaxed evening. Most storytelling is brief. It involves using concrete examples that reframe a moment by personifying human consequences. (See the sidebar "To Motivate People, Show Them How They're Helping Customers.")

People's feelings about their work are only partly about the work itself. They are equally, if not more so, about how they frame their work. Do they see what

TO MOTIVATE PEOPLE, SHOW THEM HOW THEY'RE HELPING CUSTOMERS

by Francesca Gino

Recent research points to leveraging the social aspect of work as a key factor in increasing worker motivation. In particular, interactions with the beneficiaries of one's work can be highly motivating because they heighten workers' perceptions of the impact of their work.

In one field study, Adam Grant of the Wharton School found that fundraisers who were attempting to secure scholarship donations felt more motivated when they had contact with scholarship recipients.[1] In another study, Grant found that lifeguards were more vigilant after reading stories about people whose lives have been saved by lifeguards.[2] In fact, words from the beneficiaries of one's assistance can be more motivating than those of inspirational leaders, Grant showed in another series of studies with his colleague Dave Hofmann of the University of North Carolina at Chapel Hill.[3] Similarly, when cooks see those who will be eating their food, they feel more motivated and work harder, Harvard Business School's Ryan Buell and colleagues found.

Across these studies, the key factor that improved worker motivation was a direct connection to those who benefit from one's work, including customers and clients. But this type of direct relationship can be hard

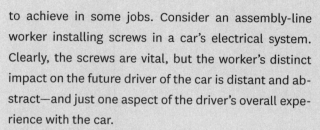

to achieve in some jobs. Consider an assembly-line worker installing screws in a car's electrical system. Clearly, the screws are vital, but the worker's distinct impact on the future driver of the car is distant and abstract—and just one aspect of the driver's overall experience with the car.

How can managers motivate such workers? By leveraging relationships that are internal to the organization. In one field study, Paul Green of Harvard Business School, Brad Staats, and I asked employees harvesting tomatoes at a tomato-processing company in California to watch a short video from a colleague within the firm telling them about the positive impact they had in the factory. Others did not watch such videos (our control condition). In the weeks after the intervention, the employees who watched a video from a colleague achieved a 7% improvement in productivity, on average, as measured by tons of tomatoes harvested per hour, relative to those in our control condition. In a follow-up laboratory study, a similar intervention increased employees' performance, because people felt a greater sense of belonging.

The existing research on motivation tells a clear story: There are both psychological and performance benefits to connecting employees to the beneficiaries of their work. As a manager, you just need to ask a

(continued)

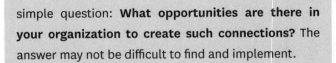

simple question: **What opportunities are there in your organization to create such connections?** The answer may not be difficult to find and implement.

_____

Francesca Gino is a behavioral scientist and the Tandon Family Professor of Business Administration at Harvard Business School. She is the author of the books _Rebel Talent: Why It Pays to Break the Rules at Work and in Life_ and _Sidetracked: Why Our Decisions Get Derailed, and How We Can Stick to the Plan_. Follow her on Twitter @francescagino.

1. Adam Grant, "Does Intrinsic Motivation Fuel the Prosocial Fire? Motivational Synergy in Predicting Persistence, Performance, and Productivity," _Journal of Applied Psychology_ 93, no. 1 (2008): 48–58.

2. Adam Grant, "The Significance of Task Significance: Job Performance Effects, Relational Mechanisms, and Boundary Conditions," _Journal of Applied Psychology_ 93, no. 1 (2008): 108–124.

3. Adam M. Grant and David A. Hofmann, "Outsourcing Inspiration: The Performance Effects of Ideological Messages from Leaders and Beneficiaries," _Organizational Behavior and Human Decision Processes_ 116, no. 2 (2011), 173–187.

Excerpted from "To Motivate Employees, Show Them How They're Helping Customers" on hbr.org, March 6, 2017 (product #H03HEY).

they're doing as a mindless ritual? Do they see it as empty compliance? Or do they see it as sacred duty? If you change the frame you change the feeling. And nothing changes frames faster than a story.

For example, in one study we did at a large healthcare provider, we examined why some employees were somewhat casual about hand hygiene while others were zealots. Handwashing in hospitals is one of the most critical factors in avoiding hospital-acquired infections. While many doctors, nurses, housekeepers, and technicians were *mostly* attentive to this innocuous act, a handful of employees were relentlessly vigilant. It turned out this group was far more likely than their peers to have *personally* been infected in the past as a patient in a hospital—or to have had a family member who was. They were motivated because they had a personal or vicarious experience with the human consequences of a seemingly simple task, and that made them *feel* differently.

It's easy to go on autopilot like Bert did. Research by A. David Smith and J. Paul Bolam shows that once a task becomes familiar, our brains devote far less cognitive resources to it. One of the downsides of this brilliant evolutionary design is that we *disconnect*. We stop seeing past our work to the people we affect.

Our company, VitalSmarts, has around 120 employees. One of our regular rituals in our monthly all-hands meeting is the *mission moment*. This is an opportunity for my colleagues and me to share stories about the impact our work has on our own lives or those of the people we serve. Recently, my colleague Mary described a conflict in her neighborhood that was escalating horribly. In a moment of clarity, she offered an apology and a cucumber from her garden rather than the next volley in the pointless fusillade. The neighbor was deeply moved by the gesture, responding with gratitude and an apology, and noting that some of what she said "was an answer to a prayer he desperately needed." I was deeply affected when Mary ended her story by saying, "None of this would have transpired the way it did had I not dug deep into the gray matter of my brain and surfaced the skills that have been my life's work."

As I later boarded a plane for a long and familiar flight to Singapore, I found an extra spring in my step. I felt I was heading toward something worthy, not simply logging miles.

In every organization we've ever studied where there was a strong sense of moral motivation, the leaders were always storytellers. They understood and acted on their responsibility to overcome the inevitable alienation of routine organizational life by connecting employees with those they serve.

———————————

Joseph Grenny is a four-time *New York Times* bestselling author, keynote speaker, and leading social scientist for business performance. His work has been translated into 28 languages, is available in 36 countries, and has generated results for 300 of the *Fortune* 500. He is the cofounder of VitalSmarts, an innovator in corporate training and leadership development.

CHAPTER 12

Help Someone Discover Work That Excites Them

by Amy Jen Su

Much has been written on a leader's role in motivating, engaging, and bringing out the best in others. Yet research suggests there is still much more that could be done. Frequently cited is the 2014 Deloitte study, which found that "up to 87% of America's workforce is not able to contribute to their full potential because they don't have passion for their work."[1] This passion gap is important because "passionate workers are committed

---

Adapted from "How to Help Someone Discover Work That Excites Them" on hbr.org, September 13, 2017 (product #H03W56).

to continually achieving higher levels of performance." Robert Kaplan, author of *What You're Really Meant to Do* states that "numerous studies of highly effective people point to a strong correlation between believing in the mission, enjoying the job, and performing at a high level." If passion plays an important role in the potential and high performance of others, how does a leader develop others toward their passions?

Adopt a Servant Leader's Mindset

In the face of heavy workloads, it's easy to have every interaction with your direct reports turn into a rushed conversation focused on getting stuff done or fixing problems. Developing others toward their passions requires a mindset shift. While many authors have written about the concept of servant leadership, one of the best definitions still comes from Robert Greenleaf, who coined the phrase in an essay called "The Servant as Leader," published in 1970. In it, Greenleaf writes, "The servant-leader is servant first . . . it begins with that natural feeling that one wants to serve. The best test, which is difficult to administer, is: Do those served grow as persons? Do they, while being served, become healthier, wiser, freer, more autonomous, more likely themselves to become servants?"

Developing the mindset of a servant leader does not mean becoming deferential or saying yes every time your team asks for something. On the contrary, it takes a strong and confident leader to be in service of a larger vision, mission, or shared purpose beyond their own agenda or ego.

To do this, servant leaders must think strategically, tying daily actions to the bigger picture. They make decisions for the good of the enterprise, not for self-preservation or to protect their own turf. They seek to understand others by asking powerful questions and listening to the answers, but also know when to provide context, direction, and guidance. Ultimately, servant leaders recognize the need to inspire individuals to work toward common goals.

Help to Unlock and Discover People's Passions

You can help to explore what drives passion on the job for your employees by giving them a chance to pause and reflect. Choose natural points in the workflow to ask questions such as:

- **In advance of new experiences:** What are you excited about for this upcoming project or initiative? What are ways you hope to develop, learn, or grow with this experience?

- **After key milestones:** What's something you felt great about or were especially proud of on that team or project? What was especially rewarding, meaningful, or inspiring coming out of that project, initiative, or event?

- **At annual performance reviews:** What did you most enjoy working on this past year and why? What are the types of things you'd like to get more experience in next year?

- **In career development conversations:** What is
your career aspiration over the next three to five
years? How do you see this role helping you get
there? What inspires you now?

Prioritize Work at the Intersection of Passion and Contribution

With greater information in hand, you can help to better
identify that sweet spot where your employee's passion
and contribution to your team or organization overlap.
In January 2017 I wrote an HBR article, "How to Prioritize Your Work When Your Manager Doesn't," about
making room for activities where passion and contribution intersect. While the article focused on how to prioritize your own work, you can apply the same framework
to helping your direct reports prioritize theirs. This en-
sures that passion is included in the equation.

Be careful of assuming that throwing more opportunities or stretch assignments at your employee is the key to
unlocking passion. At some point, this can lead to what
Michael E. Kibler calls a "brownout"—a term used to describe part of the life cycle of a star. As Kibler says, these
people "seem to be performing fine: putting in massive
hours in meetings and calls across time zones, grinding
out work while leading or contributing to global teams,
and saying all the right things in meetings. However,
these executives are often operating in a silent state of
continual overwhelm, and the predictable consequence
is disengagement."

Know When It's Time to Help Someone Move On

Practically, you aren't always going to have work or opportunities that hit the "passion-contribution" zone for your employees. The key is to recognize when a role has run its course. Don't become the boss who keeps others in a box or gets locked into a view of someone from the past. Not allowing a protégé to move on or spread their wings can create a passion drain.

One of the things that most struck me in Sydney Finkelstein's 2016 HBR article, "Secrets of the Superbosses," which was based on his review of thousands of articles and books, as well as more than 200 interviews, was how superbosses "accept churn." They recognize that "smart, creative, flexible people tend to have fast-paced careers. Even after someone moves out of their organization, superbosses continue to offer advice, personal introductions, and membership into their networks."

Helping others to develop toward their passions can be a rewarding part of being a leader. By adopting a servant leader's mindset, helping others to explore, prioritizing for passion and contribution, and supporting others' careers beyond their current role, you will have increased engagement and built long-lasting relationships.

Amy Jen Su is a cofounder and managing partner of Paravis Partners, a boutique executive coaching and leadership development firm. She is coauthor, with Muriel Maignan Wilkins, of *Own the Room: Discover Your Signature Voice to Master Your Leadership Presence* (Harvard Business Review Press, 2013). Follow her on twitter @amyjensu.

NOTES

1. John Hagel, John Seely Brown, Alok Ranjan, and Daniel Byler, "Passion at Work: Cultivating Worker Passion as a Cornerstone of Talent Development," Deloitte, October 7, 2014, https://www2.deloitte .com/insights/us/en/topics/talent/worker-passion-employee-behavior .html.

2. Michael E. Kibler, "Prevent Your Star Performers from Losing Passion for Their Work," HBR.org, January 14, 2015, https://hbr .org/2015/01/prevent-your-star-performers-from-losing-passion -in-their-work.

CHAPTER 13

How to Motivate Employees to Go Beyond Their Jobs

by Mark C. Bolino and Anthony C. Klotz

Every day, employees make decisions about whether they are willing to go the extra mile in ways that contribute to their organization's success. These are important decisions because, as research by Nathan Podsakoff and colleagues in the *Journal of Applied Psychology* shows, when employees are willing to go beyond their formal roles by helping out coworkers, volunteering to take on special assignments, introducing new ideas and work practices, attending non-mandatory meetings, putting in

---

Adapted from content posted on hbr.org, September 15, 2017 (product #H03W6D).

extra hours to complete important projects, and so forth, their companies are more efficient and effective. As a result, a critical task for successful managers is to motivate their employees to engage in these extra-role behaviors, which researchers refer to as "citizenship behaviors."

Although the benefits of citizenship behavior for organizational performance are clear, the implications for employees are more equivocal. On the one hand, many employees perform acts of citizenship because they feel committed to and connected to their peers, supervisors, and organizations. Being a good organizational citizen can also be personally and professionally rewarding because it makes work more meaningful and invigorating and contributes to better performance evaluations. On the other hand, some studies have also shown that employees sometimes feel pressured to be good organizational citizens and may do so only in order to enhance their image. Moreover, going the extra mile can deplete employees' resources, contributing to stress, work-family conflict, and citizenship fatigue. Recent research by Kai Chi Yam and colleagues suggests that employees who feel pressured to engage in citizenship may even start feeling entitled to act out by engaging in deviant behaviors. Further, while employee citizenship is often associated with positive feelings, it can also impede employees' ability to get their jobs done, which can undermine their well-being.

As this work continues, consensus is emerging that citizenship behavior tends to have negative implications when employees go above and beyond at work not because they intrinsically want to, but because they feel that they have to, or when they are unable to carry out their regular job duties and be a good citizen at the same time. Given the importance of citizenship behavior for organizational success, it is important that managers help employees find better ways to go beyond the call of duty in order to help make work more meaningful and less depleting. One potentially effective way of doing this is something we refer to as "citizenship crafting."

The idea of citizenship crafting is based on the concept of job crafting, in which people redesign their work by altering aspects of the job itself (task crafting), the people with whom they work (relationship crafting), and their mindset about their jobs (cognitive crafting) in ways that play to their strengths, motives, and passions. (Job crafting is discussed at length in chapter 16.) Whereas job crafting captures how employees redesign their formal role at work, citizenship crafting is based on the notion that employees can proactively shape the ways in which they to go beyond the call of duty such that they not only contribute to the organization, but that they are also personally meaningful, rewarding, and consistent with their strengths.

While employees are the ones who will craft their citizenship behavior, ideally they will consider not only their own needs but also those of their manager and colleagues. For this reason, we encourage managers to let their employees know what types of citizenship behaviors are most important for their work group, while recognizing that asking employees to engage in too much citizenship can be counterproductive.

Employees should also be forthright in communicating to their managers what types of citizenship behavior are most consistent with their strengths, motives, and passions. For instance, an introverted engineer who dreads socializing but does not mind pulling the occasional all-nighter might feel less obligated to take part in every social event, knowing that she can be the one to take charge when someone has to stay late to complete a critical project. Or a salesperson who cannot stand to sit through meetings, but relishes opportunities to coach others, can ask to be spared tedious committee work in exchange for making extra time to shadow and informally mentor new recruits. And employees should feel comfortable making a conscious decision to voluntarily assist their colleagues who are appreciative and generous in return, offering the type of assistance that's not such a burden to provide.

Although citizenship crafting is a new idea, prior research indicates that it should benefit employees and managers alike. First, to the extent that jobs contain tasks that align with employees' intrinsic motives, and are absent of tasks that employees feel forced to complete, research by Adam Grant has shown that job performance tends to be significantly higher; as such, citizenship crafting should result in higher quality and more impactful acts of citizenship. Second, employees who are able to engage in citizenship behaviors that play to their strengths and passions should feel less stressed and worn out from going the extra mile, according to Netta Weinstein and Richard Ryan in their article, "When Helping Helps." By realizing that not all good citizens look alike, and allowing employees to tailor their citizenship to fit their unique interests and talents, managers can simultaneously enhance employee well-being and work-group productivity. Finally, citizenship crafting should reduce the need for managers to rely on extrinsic sticks and carrots to motivate employees to go above and beyond their jobs. This should not only conserve financial resources, but given evidence that extrinsic rewards can sometimes undermine intrinsic motivation, citizenship crafting should also help employees stay internally driven to put in extra effort.

The bottom line is that managers' and employees' efforts to enhance the meaningfulness of work by redesigning employees' jobs should not stop where the formal job description ends. Instead, we encourage employees to more thoughtfully and proactively craft their citizenship behavior in ways that their extra-role contributions lead to more meaning and fulfillment while, at the same time, enhancing their firm's performance.

———————

Mark C. Bolino is the Michael F. Price Chair in International Business at the University of Oklahoma's Price College of Business. **Anthony C. Klotz** is an assistant professor of management at Oregon State University's College of Business.

Encourage Growth and Development

CHAPTER 14

To Support Learning, Managers Need to Coach

by Monique Valcour

As the previous chapter illustrated, the most powerfully motivating condition people experience at work is making progress at something that is personally meaningful. If your job involves leading others, the implications are clear: the most important thing you can do each day is to help your team members experience this progress.

Adapted from "You Can't Be a Great Manager If You're Not a Good Coach" on hbr.org, July 17, 2014 (product #H00WOP).

To do so, you must understand what drives each person, help build connections between each person's work and the organization's mission and strategic objectives, provide timely feedback, and help each person learn and grow on an ongoing basis. Regular communication around development—having *coaching conversations*—is essential. In fact, according to recent research published in the HBR.org article, "How Google Sold Its Engineers on Management," the single most important managerial competency that separates highly effective managers from average ones is coaching.

Strangely, at most companies, coaching isn't part of what managers are formally expected to do. Even though research makes it clear that employees and job candidates alike value learning and career development above most other aspects of a job, many managers don't see it as an important part of their role. Managers think they don't have the time to have these conversations, and many lack the skill. Yet 70% of employee learning and development happens on the job, not through formal training programs. So if line managers aren't supportive and actively involved, employee growth is stunted. As are engagement and retention.

Can you teach old-school, results-focused line managers to coach their employees? Absolutely. And the training boosts performance in both directions. It's a powerful experience to create a resonant connection with another person and help them to achieve something they care about and to become more of who they want to be. If there's anything an effective coaching conversation produces, it's positive energy. Hundreds of executive students have reported to me that helping others learn and grow is among the most rewarding experiences they've had as managers.

Starting today, you can be significantly more effective as a manager—and enjoy your job more—by engaging in regular coaching conversations with your team members. As you resolve to support their ongoing learning and development, here are five key tips to get you started.

Listen Deeply

Consider what it feels like when you're trying to convey something important to a person who has many things on their mind. Contrast that familiar experience with the more luxurious and deeply validating one of communicating with someone who is completely focused on you and actively listening to what you have to say with an open mind and an open heart. You can open a coaching conversation with a question such as "How would you like to grow this month?" Your choice of words is less important than your intention to clear your mind, listen with your full attention, and create a high-quality connection that invites your team member to open up and to think creatively.

Ask, Don't Tell

As a manager, you have a high level of expertise that you're used to sharing, often in a directive manner. This is fine when you're clarifying action steps for a project you're leading or when people come to you asking for advice. But in a coaching conversation, it's essential to restrain your impulse to provide the answers. Your path is not your employee's path. Open-ended questions, not answers, are the tools of coaching. You succeed as a coach by helping your team members articulate their goals and challenges and find their own answers. This is how people clarify their priorities and devise strategies that resonate with what they care about most and that they will be committed to putting into action.

Create and Sustain a Developmental Alliance

While your role as a coach is not to provide answers, supporting your team members' developmental goals and strategies is essential. Let's say that your employee mentions she'd like to develop a deeper understanding of how your end users experience the services your firm provides. In order to do so, she suggests accompanying an implementation team on a site visit next week, interviewing end users, and using the interviews to write an article on end user experience for publication on your firm's intranet-based blog. You agree that this would be valuable for both the employee and the firm. Now, make sure that you give your employee the authorization, space, and resources necessary to carry out her developmental plan. In addition to supporting her, you can also highlight her article as an example of employee-directed learning and development. Follow-up is critical to building trust and to making your coaching more effective. The more you follow through on supporting your employees' developmental plans, the more productive your coaching becomes, the greater your employees' trust in you, and the more engaged you all become. It's a virtuous cycle.

Focus On Moving Forward Positively

Oftentimes in a coaching conversation, the person you're coaching will get caught up in detailing their frustrations. "I'd love to spend more time building my network, but I have no bandwidth. I'm at full capacity just trying to stay on task with my deliverables. I'd really love to get out to some industry seminars, but I can't let myself think about it until I can get ahead of these deadlines." While it can provide temporary relief to vent, it doesn't generate solutions. Take a moment to acknowledge your employee's frustrations, but then encourage her to think about how to move past them. You might ask, "Which of the activities you mention offer the greatest potential for building your knowledge and adding value to the company?" "Could you schedule two hours of time for developmental activities each week as a recurring appointment?" "Are there skills or relationships that would increase your ability to meet your primary deliverables?" "How could we work more efficiently within the team to free up and protect time for development?"

Build Accountability

In addition to making sure you follow through on any commitments you make to employees in coaching conversations, it's also useful to build accountability for the employee's side of formulating and implementing developmental plans. Accountability increases the positive impact of coaching conversations and solidifies their rightful place as keys to organizational effectiveness. If your employee plans to research training programs that will fit his developmental goals, give these plans more weight by asking him to identify appropriate programs along with their costs and the amount of time he'll need away from work, and to deliver this information to you by a certain deadline. (And then, of course, you will need to act on the information in a timely manner.)

What will coaching your employees do for you? It will build stronger bonds between you and your team members, support them in taking ownership over their own learning, and help them develop the skills they need to perform at their peak. And it also feels good. At a coaching workshop I led last month in Shanghai, an executive said the coaching exercise he'd just participated in "felt like a bungee jump." As the workshop leader, I was delighted to observe that this man, who had arrived looking reserved and a bit tired, couldn't stop smiling for the rest of the evening. He was far from the only participant who was visibly energized by the coaching experience.

So go ahead and take the interpersonal jump. You will love the thrill of coaching conversations that catalyze your employees' growth.

———————

Monique Valcour is an executive coach, keynote speaker, and management professor. She helps clients create and sustain fulfilling and high-performance jobs, careers, workplaces, and lives. Follow her on Twitter @moniquevalcour.

CHAPTER 15

Why Talented People Don't Use Their Strengths

by Whitney Johnson

If you watch football, you've probably noticed the coaches talking to each other over headsets during the game. What you might not know is that during the 2016 season, the NFL made major league-wide improvements to its radio frequency technology, both to prevent interference from media using the same frequency and to prevent tampering. This was a development led by John Cave, VP of football technology at the National Football League. It's been incredibly helpful to the coaches. But

Adapted from content posted on hbr.org, May 8, 2018 (product #H04BEO).

it might never have been built, or at least Cave wouldn't have built it, had it not been for his boss, Michelle McKenna-Doyle, CIO of the NFL.

When McKenna-Doyle was hired, she observed that a number of her people were struggling, but not because they weren't talented—because they weren't in roles suited to their strengths. After doing a deep analysis, she started having people switch jobs. For many, this reshuffling was initially unwelcome and downright uncomfortable. Such was the case with Cave.

Cave had the talent to create products and build things. But he didn't have time to do it, because he had the big job of system development, including enterprise systems. "Why was he weighed down with the payroll system when he could figure out how to evolve the game through technology?" McKenna-Doyle asked. As she later explained to me, she envisioned a better role for his distinctive strengths. The coaches wanted to talk to each other. The technology didn't exist. She tasked Cave with creating it. "At first, he was concerned, because his overall span was shrinking. 'Just trust me,' I said. 'You're going to be a great innovator,' and he is."

Experts have long encouraged people to "play to their strengths." And why wouldn't we want to flex our strongest muscle? But based on my observations, this is easier said than done. Not because it's hard to identify what we're good at. But because we often undervalue what we inherently do well.

Often our "superpowers" are things we do effortlessly, almost reflexively, like breathing. When a boss identifies these talents and asks you to do something that uses your superpower, you may think, "But that's so easy. It's too easy." It may feel that your boss doesn't trust you to take on a more challenging assignment or otherwise doesn't value you—because you don't value your innate talents as much as you do the skills that have been hard-won.

As a leader, the challenge is not only to spot talent but also to convince your people that you value their talents and that they should, too. This is how you start to build a team of employees who bring their superpowers to work.

Begin by identifying the strengths of each member of your team. Some of my go-to questions are:

What exasperates you?

This can be a sign of a skill that comes easily to you, so much so that you get frustrated when it doesn't come naturally to others. I'm weirdly good at remembering names, for example, and often get annoyed with others who don't. I have a terrible sense of direction, however, and probably irritate other people who intrinsically sense which way is north.

What compliments do you dismiss?

When we're inherently good at something, we tend to downplay it. "Oh, it was nothing," we say—and maybe it was nothing to us. But it meant something to another person, which is why they're thanking you. Notice these moments: They can point to strengths that you underrate in yourself but are valuable to others.

What do you think about when you have nothing to think about?

Mulling over something is a sign that it matters to you. Your brain can't help but come back to it. If it matters to you that much, maybe you're good at it.

In group settings, I'll also ask people why they hired so-and-so—what that person's genius is. Rarely is this a skill listed on their résumé.

When people bring up new ideas, you can ask them, Will this leverage what you do well? Are you doing work that draws on your strengths? Are we taking on projects that make the most of your strengths?

Once each person has identified their strengths, make sure everyone remembers them. Brett Gerstenblatt, VP and creative director at CVS, has his team take a personality assessment, then post their top five strengths on their desk. Brett wants people to wear their strengths like a badge. Not to tell others why they're great, but to remind them to use their unique gifts.

Diana Newton Anderson, an entrepreneur turned social good activist, shares a story of her college basketball coach, who had her team take shots from different places on the court: the key, the elbow, the paint. He would record their percentages, and then had every person on the team memorize those percentages. This would allow the team to literally play to each other's strengths. You can do something similar with your team.

As with McKenna-Doyle, building a team that can play to their strengths begins with analysis. Observe people, especially when they are at their best. Because some will undervalue what they do well, it may be up to you to place value on what they do best. Understanding and acknowledging each person's strengths can be a team-building exercise. Then you can measure new ideas, new products, and new projects against these collective superpowers, asking: Are we playing to our strengths? When people feel strong, they are willing to venture into new territory, to play where others are not, and to consider ideas for which there isn't yet a market.

Whitney Johnson is an executive coach, speaker, and innovation thinker recently named one of the most influential management thinkers by Thinkers50. She is the author of *Build an A-Team* from Harvard Business Review Press and the critically acclaimed *Disrupt Yourself.*

CHAPTER 16

Let Employees Personalize Their Jobs

by Vivek Bapat

We live in an increasingly personalized society. We choose individualized playlists instead of radio stations. We self-select our news sources and our TV shows. Our cars have infinitely adjustable seats and telescopic steering. Everything is geared just for us.

Then we have job descriptions.

In most corporate structures today, recruitment for a position generally means starting with a formal list of tasks—the standardized job description—and hiring

---

Adapted from "Why You Should Let Employees Personalize Their Job Descriptions" on hbr.org, May 21, 2018 (product #H04BV7).

someone who can make a convincing case that they would perform each one.

As time goes on, people get stuck in these predefined roles, and, if growth opportunities aren't available, they disengage. Although concerned leaders try to address this problem in many ways—teamwork exercises, mentorship, perks, innovative office spaces, and incentive programs—their solutions miss a simple but pivotal point: Employees are engaged by engaging jobs.

In my experience leading and managing teams over two decades, I've found that job personalization—that is, fitting jobs to employees rather than fitting employees to jobs—is one of the best ways to maximize engagement.

Job personalization is another name for job crafting, a process described by Amy Wrzesniewski, Justin Berg, and Jane Dutton in their HBR article, "Turn the Job You Have into the Job You Want," as one that "involves redefining your job to incorporate your motives, strengths, and passions. The exercise prompts you to visualize the job, map its elements, and reorganize them to better suit you."

While that article tackles job crafting from an individual perspective, managers can play an important guiding role. In my experience, this approach is best applied when there are clear inflection points: when career trajectories are stalled, during corporate restructuring, or in recruiting for open positions. I've also found that it works best with individuals who bring new and growth-minded perspectives.

If you think one of your direct reports is a good candidate for job personalization, I suggest beginning the process with a true-north conversation. Ask the person to describe themselves and their career, and listen closely. What are they especially good at? What gets them excited about their career successes? What kinds of responsibilities have they not sought? Which ones did they seem to talk around or emphasize less? What you're looking for is how their skills (professional), their passions (personal), and their value (as perceived by the organization) intersect.

For these conversations to work, you need to have a growth mindset as well. (See the sidebar, "What Is a Growth Mindset?" for a better understanding of this popular but often-misunderstood term.) What is my colleague really passionate about and good at? And, more importantly, is it possible to create a role for them that accelerates their personal progression while also benefiting the organization? These conversations aren't easy and require significant self-reflection and coaching.

I've found that when creating new jobs around individuals, it is necessary to approach each situation based on the personality of the person you're trying to help. In my experience, job creation typically is best applied to three types of personas: the altruistic, the big thinkers, and the creatives. Each persona requires a different approach.

Make Helping Others a Core Responsibility for the Altruistic

In every organization, you will find a few employees who display a sense of unselfish service toward others. For example, my colleague Sylvia, who works in public

WHAT IS A GROWTH MINDSET?

by Carol Dweck

People with a fixed mindset believe that talent is a fixed quality—you either have the talent to be successful or you don't. People with a growth mindset believe that talent or ability is something you can develop through hard work, good strategies, and mentoring—that is, through learning. They tend to achieve more than those with a more fixed mindset because they worry less about looking smart and they put more energy into relishing challenges, seeking honest feedback, and learning valuable lessons from setbacks. When entire companies embrace a growth mindset, their employees report feeling far more empowered and committed; they also receive far greater organizational support for collaboration and innovation. In contrast, people at primarily fixed-mindset companies report more of only one thing: cheating and deception among employees, presumably to gain an advantage in the talent race.

"Growth mindset" has become a buzzword in many major companies, even working its way into their mission statements. But when I probe, I often discover that people's understanding of the idea is limited. Here are three common misconceptions.

1. *I already have it, and I always have.* People often confuse a growth mindset with being

flexible or open-minded or with having a positive outlook—qualities they believe they've simply always had. My colleagues and I call this a false growth mindset. Everyone is actually a mixture of fixed and growth mindsets, and that mixture continually evolves with experience. A "pure" growth mindset doesn't exist, which we have to acknowledge in order to attain the benefits we seek.

2. *A growth mindset is just about praising and rewarding effort.* This isn't true for students in schools, and it's not true for employees in organizations. In both settings, outcomes matter. Unproductive effort is never a good thing. It's critical to reward not just effort but learning and progress, and to emphasize the processes that yield these things, such as seeking help from others, trying new strategies, and capitalizing on setbacks to move forward effectively. In all of our research, the outcome—the bottom line—follows from engaging people deeply in these processes.

3. *Just espouse a growth mindset, and good things will happen.* Mission statements are wonderful things. You can't argue with lofty

(*continued*)

WHAT IS A GROWTH MINDSET?

values like growth, empowerment, or innovation. But what do they mean to employees if the company doesn't implement policies that make them real and attainable? They just amount to lip service. Organizations that embody a growth mindset (and managers who cultivate it in themselves) encourage appropriate risk-taking, knowing that some risks won't work out. They reward employees for important and useful lessons learned, even if a project does not meet its original goals. They support collaboration across organizational boundaries rather than competition among employees or units. They are committed to the growth of every member, not just in words but in deeds, such as broadly available development and advancement opportunities. And they continually reinforce growth mindset values with concrete policies.

Carol Dweck is the Lewis & Virginia Eaton Professor of Psychology at Stanford University and the author of *Mindset: The New Psychology of Success*.

Adapted from "What Having a 'Growth Mindset' Actually Means" on hbr .org, January 13, 2016 (product #H02LQX).

relations, often goes out of her way to welcome and mentor new colleagues.

Altruistic individuals like Sylvia may not hold formal power, but they are well respected by their colleagues and have a lot of influence as a result.

Leaders can help these employees by making their "fringe" activities a core part of their job responsibilities. After I had a true-north discussion with Sylvia, for example, it was clear that her innate skills in networking, presenting, facilitating, and mentoring could provide a lot of value for the company, which had just initiated a new leadership development program. In this case, Sylvia's passion aligned with the goals of the organization, so we jointly crafted a roadmap for Sylvia to learn more about leadership development and gain career counseling skills—all while pursuing her current role in PR.

Establish Clear Goals for the Big Thinkers

While every organization wants big thinkers on their teams, it's no secret that big thinkers struggle with the traditional organizational constructs that can stifle their ideas. Big thinkers are dreamers and might typically struggle with details, trivial conversations, organizational politics, processes, and decision flows. While these innovators are natural candidates for job personalization, leaders should design clear goals—as well as a safety net that allows for failure.

This was the story with Amanda. After her position was lost in a reshuffling, I invited Amanda to join my team. Having worked with her on other projects, I knew that she was passionate about bold ideas. Unfortunately, because she had found herself in tactical, traditional roles, many others found her ideas to be too far-fetched, impractical, or politically incorrect. After having a true-north discussion, Amanda and I realized that her passion and skills aligned best with the topic of corporate purpose.

This was a big area to explore, so the key was to establish clear goals. Since Amanda was flying solo, in a sense, we created an outreach program to identify like-minded individuals with a similar passion across different parts of the company—from sales, to product development, to services. We ideated constantly.

We had several setbacks and failures. But, over time, the ideas resonated with many employees, and people began contributing to the initiative, going above and beyond their day jobs. Over time, the team created an informal purpose-driven network to keep the collaboration growing. All these actions were finally amplified and recognized when the company decided to make purpose a central theme of its brand strategy. Amanda is now a recognized and sought-after leader in her own right.

Create New Positions for the Creatives

Creativity is the heartbeat of progress. Yet, as organizations develop over time, even the jobs that require the most creative thinking tend to become fixed and rigid. When recruiting for these areas, leaders can create new opportunities for individuals by exercising flexibility in co-defining roles for creatives that are synched with their creative vision of the future.

Recently a member of my team left to take on a different position in the company. As we interviewed for a replacement, we found many candidates who looked to be perfect matches for the position as described, but very few had a clear-eyed view about what the position could be.

Joe wasn't a perfect fit on paper, but during the interview process he painted a new creative vision, different from the one we had before. Ultimately, we created a new position that was custom designed for that vision, and also harmonized with where the team was going.

Of course, molding jobs to people can't result in everyone taking on plum tasks and rejecting the others, or disengaging entirely and rejecting them all like Bartleby the scrivener in the famous short story by Herman Melville, whose response to every request is, "I would prefer not to." That's where management skill comes in: Across the team we create a blend of responsibilities that gets everything done. We customize without catering to prima donnas.

And some jobs clearly do not lend themselves to molding around the person. A position operating a particular piece of equipment or exercising a particular skill does not allow for much latitude, which is perhaps why those types of jobs are the ones most rapidly lost to advanced AI and robotics.

Millions of jobs, though, are not fixed—we just treat them as if they are. Rather than simply handing an employee the same set of tasks his or her predecessor had done, managers at every level need to fine-tune. As the Wharton professor Peter Cappelli has recognized about retention, the new art of management is built around personalization.

Workplace customization has its challenges. It's a lot easier to draw an org chart and expect every hire to fill a box. It can be particularly uncomfortable when adding a new team member, especially if tasks and responsibilities trickle down to other team members. And even as you customize, you need to see the big picture—the most engaging job for some people may simply not help meet larger goals, in which case there's a fundamental mismatch.

Over time, however, job personalization will create more effective teams. It will allow managers to place a premium on hiring for talent and intelligence despite some possible gaps in experience. And, I believe, the Gallup pollsters will find that it will change the direction of employee engagement.

———————

Vivek Bapat is the SVP and head of marketing and communications strategy at SAP. He partners with senior business leaders and global influencers to develop brand, content, customer, and employee engagement strategies with impact. Follow him on Twitter @vivek_bapat.

CHAPTER 17

Mentoring Someone Who Doesn't Know What Their Career Goals Should Be

by Tania Luna and Jordan Cohen

"Tell me about your career goals." How often have you said this to a person you're managing or mentoring, only to get a blank stare in return? Perhaps the person confides that they don't know what their goals should be, or

---

Adapted from "How to Mentor Someone Who Doesn't Know What Their Career Goals Should Be" on hbr.org, July 10, 2018 (product #H04FHV).

even whether there are opportunities to advance at your company. How do you begin to provide support?

Career dissatisfaction is a growing challenge in today's world, which is why we've decided to do things differently at WW (formerly known as Weight Watchers), with the help of LifeLabs Learning. The results of CEB's 2015 employee survey capture the problem well: 70% of employees surveyed (across many industries) reported being dissatisfied with career opportunities at their company—a disturbing figure given that it is one of the biggest drivers of engagement and retention. At the same time, 75% of organizations said they expected to face a shortage of necessary skills and knowledge among their employees. So, on the one hand, employees feel they can't advance fast enough, and on the other, companies believe employees are growing too slowly. How can such a blatant and dangerous contradiction exist? And what can we do about it?

Before offering solutions, we'd like to propose a radical diagnosis: The problem lives not in a lack of career opportunities, but rather in the very concept of a career. We are suffering from the *career myth*—a delusional belief in the outdated idea of linear career progression.

Consider the etymology of the word "career." It comes from the 16th-century word for "road." When we envision a career, we imagine a direct path with a final destination. And not long ago, this concept was useful. Career growth meant attaining incremental increases in prestige and compensation. You could look at the past and use it as a gauge of the future—taking the steps that others took to get to where they got. This vision of career growth no longer matches reality. We no longer need to be good at predicting the future; we now have to succeed when the future is unpredictable. We have to abandon the career myth and create a new framework for personal and professional growth.

Let's return to the employee who needs direction and feels stuck and confused about their career. If you can't point them toward a reassuring career ladder, what can you do to support their growth and increase their impact on the company? Here are some of the steps we're taking at WW to help employees move beyond the career myth:

Dispel the Career Myth

First we tell employees that it is fine and even preferable not to have a concrete career path in mind. Being overly attached to a specific path can turn into a *career trap*, blinding us to nonlinear opportunities for growth. We recently launched biannual growth conversations between managers and employees. Rather than job titles, employees discuss experiences, responsibilities, and lifestyle changes they might want.

Good questions to ask:

- "What problems excite you?"

- "What strengths can you build on?"

- "What types of work do you want to do less of and more of?"

- "What would you do differently if you quit your career?"

Focus on Transferable Skills

We train our managers to help their direct reports develop transferable skills, not climb a ladder. These are skills that increase employability because they can be applied to a variety of roles and situations now and in the future (for example, communication, self-management, writing, public speaking). Rather than investing in one path, we tell employees, they should diversify their career capital. To provide some direction, we also want managers to advertise the skills that are most wanted on the team.

Good questions to ask:

- "Of the skills we're looking to grow on the team or in the company, which interest you most?"

- "What skills would help you gain more influence in your current role?"

- "What skill gaps are standing in your way or holding you back?"

Create Milestones

One of the perks of an old-school career is the title progression that delineates advancement. As organizations become flatter, and growth nonlinear, we have to put extra effort into making milestones that mark progress. One way we've done this is to create badges that demarcate growth. For example, when managers receive training, they receive a certificate. To get their next badge, they must complete an advanced program. A badge system can demarcate skills, knowledge, and achievements—creating a portfolio of accomplishments rather than a traditional résumé. Another milestone solution we've implemented is a quarterly conversation focused on tracking goals employees set for themselves, aligned with companywide priorities. Next, we'll develop more visible recognition platforms so that employees can celebrate their accomplishments and share their knowledge.

Good questions to ask:

- "What do you want to achieve next? How will you know you've achieved it?"

- "Let's gamify this goal. What's level one? How about level two?"

- "What do you want to name this next milestone?"

- "How might you share what you've learned?"

Encourage Small Experiments

The growing complexity and unpredictability of work means we need to run many small experiments to discover what suits us best. To fuel a spirit of experimentation, we've launched opportunities for employees across the world to get training in topics they are curious to explore. We're also helping managers encourage experiments among their reports and equipping them with skills to give clear, actionable feedback on their reports' progress.

Good questions to ask:

- "What areas of the business intrigue you?"

- "How might you design a short experiment to test your interest level?"

- "Who might you want to collaborate with?"

- "What have you discovered about yourself from your past experiments?"

The scary thing about acknowledging that the career myth exists is admitting that you don't know what comes next. The wonderful thing about it is realizing that every experience you've collected thus far has merit. Every job you've held and every relationship you've forged is a kind of key that can unlock a future opportunity. The keys don't have to make sense together. There doesn't need to be a clear, linear narrative to explain how you got from A to B. And if your employees still worry that they don't have a clear path in mind, lean on the wisdom of Lewis Carroll, in this paraphrasing of a passage from *Alice in Wonderland*: "If you don't know where you are going, any road will get you there."

Tania Luna is a partner at the leadership training company LifeLabs Learning. She is a psychology researcher, TED speaker, and coauthor of the book *Surprise: Embrace the Unpredictable and Engineer the Unexpected*. **Jordan Cohen** is Vice President, People—U.S. at WW (formerly Weight Watchers International). He is an expert on knowledge worker productivity.

CHAPTER 18

How to Retain and Engage Your B Players

by Liz Kislik

We've heard for decades that we should only hire A players, and should even try to cut non-A players from our teams. But not only do the criteria for being an A player vary significantly by company; it's unrealistic to think you can work only with A players. Further, as demonstrated by Google's Aristotle project, a study of what makes teams effective, this preference for A players ignores the deep value that the people you may think of as B players actually provide.

Adapted from content posted on hbr.org, September 19, 2018 (product #H04JJF).

As I've seen in companies of all sizes and industries, stars often struggle to adapt to the culture, and may not collaborate well with colleagues. B players, on the other hand, are often less concerned about their personal trajectories, and are more likely to go above and beyond in order to support customers, colleagues, and the reputation of the business. For example, when one of my clients went through a disastrous changeover from one enterprise resource planning system to another, it was someone perceived as a B player who kept all areas of the business informed as she took personal responsibility for ensuring that every transaction and customer communication was corrected.

How can you support your B players to be their best and contribute the most possible, rather than wishing they were A players? Consider these five approaches to stop underestimating your B players and help them to reach their potential.

Get to know and appreciate them as the unique individuals they are

This is the first step to drawing out their hidden strengths and skills. Learn about their personal concerns, preferences, and the way they see and go about their work. Be sure you're not ignoring them because they're introverts, remote workers, or don't know how to be squeaky wheels. A senior leader I worked with had such a strong preference for extroverts that she ignored or downgraded team members who were just going about their business.

Meanwhile, the stars on her team got plenty of attention and resources, even though they often created drama and turmoil, rather than carrying their full share of responsibility for outcomes. Some of the team members she thought of as B players started turning over after long-term frustration. When the leader and several of her stars eventually left the company, some of the B's came back and were able to make significant contributions because they supported the mission and understood the work processes.

Reassess job fit

Employees rarely do their best if they're in jobs that highlight their weaknesses rather than their strengths. They may have technical experience but no interest, or they could be weak managers but strong individual contributors. One leader I know had been growing increasingly more frustrated and less effective; the pressures of satisfying the conflicting demands of different departments were too much for her. Then she took a lateral move to manage a smaller, more cohesive team concentrating on developing new products, and was able to focus and be inspirational again once she was freed from the pressures of managing projects in such a political environment.

Consider the possibility of bias in your assignments

Women and people of color are often overlooked for challenging or high-status assignments. They're assumed "not to be ready," or they're not considered because they don't act like commonly held but stereotyped views of "leaders." When a midlevel leader who was trying to get more exposure and advancement for one of his team members couldn't figure out what was holding her back in the eyes of a senior leader, I raised this possibility, and we strategized multiple ways that her boss could showcase the quality and impact of her work in upcoming meetings.

Intentionally support them to be their best

Some people are their own worst critics, or have deep-seated limiting beliefs that hold them back. When one of my clients lost a senior leader and couldn't afford to replace her at market rates, a longtime B player near the end of his career nervously filled the gap. Although he expanded his duties and kept the team going, he emphasized to both his management and himself that he wasn't really up to the job, and most of the executive team continued to treat him that way. It was not until after he had retired, and someone new had to fill his shoes, that it became clear how much he had done on the organization's behalf. The executive team never came to grips with how much more he could have accomplished had they provided the necessary development, support, and appreciation all along.

Give permission to take the lead

In 30 years of practice, one of the most common reasons I've seen people hold back is if they don't believe they've been given permission to step up. (The people we think of as A's tend not to ask for or wait for permission.) Some B players aren't comfortable in the spotlight, but they thrive when they're encouraged to complete a mission or to contribute for the good of the company. A midlevel leader I coach is quiet, modest, and doesn't like to make waves. She kept waiting for her new leader to lay out a vision for the future and to provide direction about how the work should be done. I asked what she would do if she was suddenly in charge. She laid out a cogent plan, and I encouraged her to present it to the new leader and ask for permission to proceed. Now she and the senior leader are moving forward in partnership.

We can't all be A players, and it's unrealistic to think we'll only ever work with A players. But that may not be the appropriate goal. Instead, try using these strategies to help employees give their best, and you'll be ensuring that your whole team can turn in an A+ performance.

Liz Kislik helps organizations from the *Fortune* 500 to national nonprofits and family-run businesses solve their thorniest problems. She has taught at NYU and Hofstra University, and recently spoke at TEDxBaylorSchool. You can download her free guide, "How to Resolve Interpersonal Conflicts in the Workplace," at lizkislik.com.

CHAPTER 19

What to Do When a Good Employee Stops Trying to Grow

by Whitney Johnson

The best managers know they're supposed to give the people they lead challenging assignments to keep them interested and engaged. But what do you do when someone you manage gets to the top of their learning curve—and doesn't really want to be pushed any further?

As a manager, you might feel relieved that someone so valuable seems happy to stay where they are. There is

Adapted from content posted on hbr.org, August 24, 2018 (product #H04HJS).

a common mindset that favors leaving high-performing employees in place once they have mastered their domain, indefinitely reaping the rewards of their labor, but it ultimately has a downside.

Think of the difference between a stagnant pond—unmoving, algae-covered, a breeding ground for mosquitoes—and a lively, bubbling stream. In the stream, there's enough motion to keep the water fresh.

Employees at the high end of their learning curve also require change. They are settling into a comfort zone, and absent the stimuli associated with overcoming challenges and building competence, they can quickly become bored, indifferent, and disengaged. Stagnation can breed entitlement, an environment hostile to creative thinking and innovation.

I see this happen for one of two reasons: the need for a new challenge, or the need for a change.

As managers, we can use this insight to figure out which approach to take. There are really two options here.

Offer a Stretch Assignment

That's what Sumeet Shetty, product development manager at SAP India, did. Following a reorganization, he inherited a new team. Some of these people made it clear they were happy right where they were—they were comfortable, settled into their routine. But Shetty saw that they were capable of more.

So he gave them stretch assignments, including an exercise in which they had to rehearse board report speeches over and over again. They complained that rehearsing for a board presentation was unnecessary. And their first tries reflected these sentiments—they really weren't very good. But by the sixth time, the presentations were improving. And when the team reported back at the end of the year on Shetty's performance, they cited this stretch assignment as the most impactful thing he had done as a manager. Six months earlier he had been desperate to find a way to stop the complaining. And finding a professional solution was not easy, but ultimately ended up being what they needed.

Encourage an Entirely New Learning Curve

If your employees' current level of skill is high but not growing, suggest a move to a new assignment, new team, or a new project or client—anything to help them jump to a new learning curve. When people hang out at the top, their mastery can prevent others who are ready to grow from doing so.

Be direct and sympathetic as you communicate their successes and growth. They've simply outgrown their current position.

Recently, one of my coaching clients had this very conversation: They encouraged a good employee to leave the team. Now, this was a valued employee who had been in the organization for over a decade. My client wasn't going to kick him to the curb. But it had become clear—to both my client and the employee—that the employee had stalled in his current role. It was a tough conversation, but both parties walked away with a huge sense of relief. The employee, no longer feeling stuck, ultimately jumped into a highly entrepreneurial endeavor for two years, then chose to retire. He got his swan song and a strong finish.

Managing this way isn't easy. Shanna Hocking, associate vice president of development at the Children's Hospital of Philadelphia, speaks highly of her former boss Pam Parker, VP for advancement at the University of Alabama. Parker was tough, and she pushed Hocking on to new learning curves and helped her see when she needed to leap to a new challenge.

Now Hocking is the boss and hopes to emulate Parker's style. She's realized that investing in employees involves parting with something—her time, effort, and mental energy. It won't work for people who are focused on instant gratification and whose strategy doesn't encompass anything beyond the next quarterly report. The dividends will come, but true development doesn't happen in days or months; it can take years and sometimes even decades.

When we have experts on our teams, it's not about stepping back and letting them "float." It's time to offer an assignment that really stretches them, or else to encourage them to move on. Instead of dreading these types of difficult conversations, think of them as a great time to express your appreciation and encouragement. Every employee, however long they've worked for you, wants to know they matter. Nothing says that quite like giving them the opportunity to grow.

Whitney Johnson is an executive coach, speaker, and innovation thinker recently named one of the most influential management thinkers by Thinkers50. She is the author of *Build an A-Team* from Harvard Business Review Press and the critically acclaimed *Disrupt Yourself*.

Prevent Burnout on Your Team

CHAPTER 20

One in Five Highly Engaged Employees Is at Risk of Burnout

by Emma Seppala and Julia Moeller

Dorothea loved her new workplace and was highly motivated to perform. Her managers were delighted with her high engagement, professionalism, and dedication. She worked long hours to ensure that her staff was properly managed, that her deadlines were met, and that her team's work was nothing short of outstanding. In the first two months, she single-handedly organized a large

Adapted from content published on hbr.org, February 2, 2018 (product #H044XI).

conference—marketing and organizing all the details of the conference and filling it to capacity. It was a remarkable feat.

In the last weeks prior to the event, however, she was so stressed out that she couldn't sleep and began to feel physically and emotionally exhausted and even depressed. She was instructed to take time off work. She missed the conference and needed a long recovery before reaching earlier levels of performance and well-being. Her burnout symptoms had resulted from stress and the depletion of her resources over time.

Engagement means flourishing, or does it?

Employee engagement is a major concern for HR leaders. Year after year, concerned managers and researchers discuss Gallup's shocking statistic that seven out of ten U.S. employees report feeling unengaged. Figuring out how to increase employee engagement has been a burning question for companies and consultants across the board.

As described throughout this book, the many positive outcomes of engagement include greater productivity and quality of work, increased safety, and higher retention rates. These outcomes are in fact so well established that some researchers like Arnold Bakker, professor of work and organizational psychology at the Erasmus University Rotterdam, and colleagues have linked engagement to the experience of "flourishing at work." Similarly, Amy L. Reschly, Professor of Educational Psychology at the University of Georgia, and colleagues concluded that student engagement at schools was a sign of "flourishing."

While engagement certainly has its benefits, most of us will have noticed that, when we are highly engaged in working toward a goal we can also experience something less than positive: high levels of stress. Here's where things get more complicated.

A recent study, called the Emotion Revolution in the Workplace, conducted by the Yale Center for Emotional Intelligence, in collaboration with the Faas Foundation, has cast doubts on the idea of engagement as a purely beneficial experience. This survey examined the levels of engagement and burnout in over 1,000 U.S. employees. For some people, engagement is indeed a purely positive experience; two out of five employees in our survey reported high engagement and low burnout. These employees also reported high levels of positive outcomes (such as feeling positive emotions and acquiring new skills) and low negative outcomes (such as feeling negative emotions or looking for another job). We'll call these the optimally engaged group.

However, the data also showed that one out of five employees reported both high engagement *and* high burnout. We'll call this group the engaged-exhausted group. These engaged-exhausted workers were passionate about their work, but also had intensely mixed feelings about it—reporting high levels of interest, stress, and frustration. While they showed desirable behaviors such as high skill acquisition, these apparent model employees also reported the highest turnover intentions in our sample—even higher than the unengaged group.

That means that companies may be at risk of losing some of their most motivated and hardworking employees not for a *lack* of engagement, but because of their simultaneous experiences of high stress and burnout symptoms.

How to maintain high engagement without burning out in the process

While most HR efforts have stayed centered around the question of how to promote employee engagement only, we need to start taking a more nuanced approach and ask how to promote engagement while avoiding burning out employees in the process. Here's where key differences we found between the optimally engaged and the engaged-exhausted employees can shed some light.

Half of the optimally engaged employees reported having *high resources*, such as supervisor support, rewards and recognition, and self-efficacy at work, but *low demands* such as low workload, low cumbersome bureaucracy, and low to moderate demands on concentration and attention. In contrast, such experiences of high resources and low demands were rare (4%) among the engaged-exhausted employees, the majority of whom (64%) reported experiencing *high demands and high resources*.

This provides managers and supervisors with a hint as to where they can start supporting employees for optimal engagement. In order to promote engagement, it is crucial to provide employees with the resources they need to do their job well, feel good about their work, and recover from work-related stressors.

Many HR departments, knowing employees are feeling the pressure, offer wellness programs on combating stress—usually through healthy eating, exercise, or mindfulness. Our data suggests that while wellness initiatives can be helpful, a much bigger lever is the work itself. It's up to managers to monitor the level of demands they're placing on people, as well as the balance between demands and resources. The higher the work demands, the higher employees' need for support, acknowledgment, or opportunities for recovery. (See the sidebar, "Are You Protecting Your Stars from Flaming Out?")

What about stretch goals? Challenge, we're told, is motivating. While that can be true, we too often forget that high challenges tend to come at high cost, and that challenging achievement situations cause not only anxiety and stress even for the most motivated individuals, but also lead to states of exhaustion. And the research on stretch goals is mixed—for a few people, chasing an ambitious goal does lead to higher performance than pursuing a moderate one. In most cases, though, a stretch goal leads us to become demotivated, take foolish risks, or quit.

Managers and HR leaders can help employees by dialing down the demands they're placing on people—ensuring that employee goals are realistic and rebalancing the workloads of employees who, by virtue of being particularly skilled or productive, have been saddled with too much. They can also try to increase the resources available to employees; this includes not only material resources such as time and money, but intangible resources such as empathy and friendship, and letting employees disengage from work when they're not working. By avoiding emailing people after hours, setting a norm

ARE YOU PROTECTING YOUR STARS
FROM FLAMING OUT?

by Matt Plummer

We're familiar with the story. A high-performing employee takes on a new opportunity at work, only to find himself ill and burned out shortly after. This isn't an unusual experience for high performers: A five-year study by Awbery Management Centre, a U.K.-based consultancy, found that 20% of the top-performing leaders of U.K. businesses are affected by corporate burnout.

It's easy to blame burnout on the high performers themselves. After all, the stereotype is that these over-achievers say yes to more work even when they're at capacity. They routinely put work first, canceling personal engagements to finish the job.

While such habits may be partially to blame, this isn't the full story. In my experience, many companies and leaders engage in three common practices, often unknowingly, that make top performers more likely to burn out:

They put high performers on the hardest projects. It makes sense: Of course you'd want your best people on the most important projects. But if you keep going back to the same small group of people time and time again, you'll run the risk of wearing them out.

They use high performers to compensate for weaker team members. Lisa is a high performer at a leading consulting firm. She says: "You're seen as an exemplary employee, so you're expected to support lower performers and mentor others." While many star performers do enjoy coaching others, they understandably start to feel resentful if they think the boss is letting poor performers off the hook.

They ask high performers to help on many small efforts unrelated to their work. Star performers are often enlisted to complete one-off tasks because of their aptitude with particular skills—making powerful slides or navigating WordPress, for instance. While this issue is often framed as the individual's problem, because they didn't set clear boundaries or say no, it's more fairly seen as an organizational problem where the most hardworking people are "rewarded" with more work.

Managers must become more aware of how these practices are affecting people and look to scale them back when possible. I recommend three other strategies to help employers and leaders support high performers over the long term:

(continued)

ARE YOU PROTECTING YOUR STARS FROM FLAMING OUT?

Let high performers occasionally pick their projects. High performers generally are very motivated by the work. Yet, they don't regularly get the option to do the projects they care most about unless they happen to also be the hardest projects available, or they agree to do something on top of their normal work. Letting them choose some of their projects reconnects them with the reason they are excited to do their job—something that can get lost in the throes of burnout.

Create high-performing pairs. High performers routinely find themselves separated from those they most closely relate to and enjoy working with. This happens for obvious reasons, but surrounding them with low performers increases their workload, saps their morale, and limits their development. Pairing two stars of *a similar level* can help distribute added weight and improve both people's experience without robbing teams of their high performers.

Keep track of additional demands on their time. Demands unrelated to core work are unsuspected drivers of burnout because they feel insignificant in isolation and it's hard to keep track of their aggregate effect. Simply keeping track of all requests in a single place can equiphigh performers with the awareness to turn some down.

High performers hold great value for any company, delivering 400% more productivity than average performers, according to research by Ernest O'Boyle and Herman Aguinis. Companies will lose much of this value if they don't take deliberate action to protect their high performers from burnout.

———

Matt Plummer is the founder of Zarvana, which offers online programs and coaching services to help working professionals become more productive by developing time-saving habits. Before starting Zarvana, Matt spent six years at the Bridgespan Group. Follow him on Twitter @mtplummer.

Adapted from "How Are You Protecting Your High Performers from Burnout?" on hbr.org, June 21, 2018 (product #H04ETX).

that evenings and weekends are work-free, and encouraging a regular lunch break in the middle of the day, leaders can make sure they're sending a consistent message that balance matters.

The data is clear: Engagement is key, and it's what we should strive for as leaders and employees. But what we want is *smart* engagement—the kind that leads to enthusiasm, motivation and productivity, without the burnout. Increased demands on employees need to be balanced with increased resources—particularly before important deadlines and during other times of stress.

———————

Emma Seppala, PhD, is the science director of Stanford University's Center for Compassion and Altruism Research and Education and author of *The Happiness Track.* She is also founder of Fulfillment Daily. Follow her on Twitter @emmaseppala or her website emma seppala.com. **Julia Moeller, PhD,** is an assistant professor at the University of Leipzig, Germany, and consultant for the Yale Center for Emotional Intelligence. She studies motivation and emotions in schools and workplaces, with a focus on mixed feelings. Follow her on Twitter @passionresearch.

CHAPTER 21

Your Overwhelmed, Stressed-Out Team Needs Relief

By Julie Mosow

Is your team stressed out? These days, everyone seems overwhelmed and way too busy. But even when your team members have a lot on their plates, they don't have to sacrifice their health or happiness. What can you do to reduce your team's stress? How can you help them focus on what really needs to get done?

Adapted from "Help Your Overwhelmed, Stressed-Out Team" on hbr.org, January 16, 2015 (product #H01TS5).

What the Experts Say

As a leader, it's your job to help your people find balance. Of course, you need results, but you also want a team that's not at constant risk of burning out. Research by Clifford Nass, Eyal Ophir, and Anthony Wagner shows that memory, attention, and concentration suffer when people try to manage the constant stream of communication and distraction that's a regular part of the workplace. Julie Morgenstern, productivity expert and author of *Never Check E-Mail in the Morning*, sees this every day: "Almost everyone struggles to focus at work," she says. "We want to think, write, and strategize, but because these functions require deep thinking and uninterrupted time, we stay busy with the tasks, meetings, and messages that pop up all day long rather than tackling really important projects." Liane Davey, vice president of team solutions at Knightsbridge Human Capital and author of *You First*, agrees, noting that an overly busy office can kill morale and leave employees disengaged and less capable of getting things done. It's on you, the manager, to help your people cut through the chaos, reduce stress, and make sure your team can accomplish its most important work.

Focus your team on the things that matter

The first step, says Davey, is to identify the unique contribution your team makes to the organization. Begin by asking, "What does the company expect from my team that no other group can accomplish?" Don't answer this alone in your office. Involve your team. Once you all agree on your team's purpose, it becomes the guiding principle for how everyone should spend their time and the litmus test for what work team members should take on and what they should let go.

Edit their workload

Evaluate each project based on whether or not it's in what Davey calls "the sweet spot"—what you've previously identified as your group's unique purpose, what they're good at, and what's important to the larger goals of the organization. "It's the manager's responsibility to develop an action plan that allows everyone to be more productive and to insulate their teams from low-priority work that may trickle down from senior management," she says. When a new assignment comes your way, don't automatically say yes. "Remember to consider each project with an eye to whether or not it takes advantage of what your team, and only your team, has to offer," Morgenstern says.

Schedule uninterrupted work

"When you get distracted by something at work," says Morgenstern, "it takes at least 20 minutes to refocus on the task at hand." Encourage your team to set aside an hour or more (Morgenstern's team devotes three hours) each morning for quiet, proactive work. "Be sure everyone understands that there are to be no interruptions unless it's an emergency," she recommends. By making it a group goal, you increase your collective focus and prevent backsliding. Also check that your team members know how to break larger projects up into smaller tasks that can be accomplished in the amount of time you've set aside for strategic work each day. "Once they use this time effectively," she says, "their productivity will improve."

Fix your meetings

Meetings can be a huge waste of time," says Davey. To avoid that problem, "every meeting should include standing agenda items to allow for productive discussions and decision making about the team's core assignments," she says. Morgenstern suggests that managers establish no more than three objectives, decide who needs to be there, set limits on the duration of meetings, and use the last 15 minutes to clarify how the participants will move forward. Above all, make sure a meeting is really necessary. "Sometimes an email or memo can accomplish the same goal in a much shorter amount of time," she suggests.

Set limits on email

Technology has created an always-on culture, where work bleeds into evenings and weekends. But that can be counterproductive if your people never feel they have a break. Morgenstern suggests setting boundaries on the workday and limiting after-hours emails to urgent issues. "So many people are addicted to their phones, but over time, most realize that there's very little that can't wait and that it's far more important to connect to what's meaningful to us both personally and professionally," she says. The brain is actually wired for rest, adds Davey. "Without taking time to recharge, we create unsustainable levels of stress and anxiety."

Lead by example

When setting new norms for your team, you need to walk the talk yourself. "The movement against busy starts at the top," Davey says, pointing to the way Jeff Weiner of LinkedIn schedules time for what he calls "nothing." Talk to your team about what you're doing and why, Morgenstern recommends, and if one of your strategies isn't working, admit it, try something different (see more suggestions from executive coach Monique Valcour in the sidebar, "Tips for Fighting Burnout on Your Team"), and move on. Show that you're committed to making a change both individually and as a group. "It takes a while to break these habits," she says, "but once you all get used to a deeper sense of accomplishment, you'll never go back."

Principles to Remember

Do:

- Agree on what's unique about your group's skills and experience.

- Reduce or eliminate assignments that don't align with your team's purpose.

- Schedule time for high-level, strategic work.

Don't:

- Email your employees at all hours—set limits on technology use.

TIPS FOR FIGHTING BURNOUT ON YOUR TEAM

by Monique Valcour

Burnout is rarely an individual phenomenon; fixing and preventing it requires leadership. You can help your team thrive by implementing the following advice.

Watch for Warning Signs

- The signs of burnout are obvious in some people but subtle in others. Keep an eye out for tiredness, lack of focus, depressed mood, hostility, and expressions of hopelessness.

- Regularly check in with team members to gauge their physical, cognitive, and emotional energy levels.

Set Limits on Workloads

- Talk to your team about its collective capacity, and ensure that assignments and deadlines don't exceed it.

- Shield your team from external pressures, including unreasonable or unclear client and management demands.

Insist on Renewal

- Communicate that optimal performance depends on rest and renewal. Encourage people to set sensible limits on work hours.

- Set an example by keeping reasonable hours yourself.

- Make sure your team members take their full vacation time.

Boost Control

- Clarify expectations; grant flexibility on where, when, and how people get work done.

- Advocate for the resources your team needs to perform.

- Create uninterrupted time for people to make progress on important tasks.

Make Recognition Meaningful

- Regularly highlight wins and successes, even small ones.

- Recognize and reward people for helping others.

- Note the positive impact of your team's work on others.

Emphasize Learning

- Routinely ask team members about their development goals and what resources are required to achieve them.

(continued)

TIPS FOR FIGHTING BURNOUT ON YOUR TEAM

- Share what you're learning and how you're doing it.

Facilitate Mutual Support

- Talk regularly about progress toward team goals.

- At team meetings, ask what assistance people need and can offer one another.

- Be open about asking for and giving support.

Build Community

- Don't tolerate incivility on your team. Set an example for respectful, compassionate behavior toward others.

- Encourage people to share what's happening in their lives outside of work.

Monique Valcour is an executive coach, keynote speaker, and management professor. She helps clients create and sustain fulfilling and high-performance jobs, careers, workplaces, and lives. Follow her on Twitter @moniquevalcour.

Excerpted from *Harvard Business Review*, November 2016 (product #R1611H).

- Call meetings without an explicit purpose—stick to an agenda.

- Underestimate the importance of your own behavior—you set the norms on your team.

Case Study: Make Time for Your Most Important Work

"Our employees were really struggling to manage their workload," says Steven Handmaker, chief marketing officer at Assurance, an independent insurance brokerage. Too many emails, too many meetings, and too many interruptions had brought everyone to their breaking point. Management decided to bring in a consultant to help. His recommendation: implement priority-work time.

Every employee at every level was encouraged to schedule a certain number of hours to complete important projects. "The consultant suggested 15 hours per week," Steven says, "which was a huge shock."

Nevertheless, the leadership team, including Assurance's CEO, began scheduling priority-work time in their calendars, and employees enthusiastically followed suit. "It took about six months for the entire company to get used to the new system," Steven says. Most employees now have eight to ten hours on their calendars blocked off each week, and everyone is responsible for supporting their colleagues and employees in doing the same. If Steven sees that his team isn't planning and using priority-work time, it's his responsibility to speak to them and find out why.

How successful has priority-work time been? "What we know for sure," says Steven, "is that our employees are happier. We've received awards from *Fortune*, the *Chicago Tribune*, and from industry organizations for being a great place to work. But we also see internally that the rapid adoption of this practice means that it's been successful. We respect how hard everyone works, and part of that is simply letting people do their jobs."

Julie Mosow is a freelance editor and writer as well as the lead editorial consultant at Marly Rusoff & Associates.

CHAPTER 22

How to Apply the Right Amount of Pressure

By Liane Davey

While the popular press talks of stress as a negative to be avoided, seasoned managers know better. If you're trying to drum up new business, get a customer's order out on time, or hit your numbers for the quarter, a little stress goes a long way. It's even more important when you're trying to transform your business or revitalize a sagging culture. That's when you need enough stress to motivate action.

Adapted from "How to Put the Right Amount of Pressure on Your Team" on hbr.org, July 1, 2016 (product #H02ZLT).

In its most positive form, stress results when an employee tries to do the same old things in a new environment. Those out-of-date behaviors produce subpar results and the growing gap in performance creates tension. It's exactly the kind of stress you want, because it counteracts the powerful inertia of habit.

If you've been around the management block a time or two, you've probably also seen the other side of stress. As stress gets too high, instead of increasing momentum it can counterintuitively start to decrease it. You can immobilize people with too much stress: You stifle the creativity required to come up with new ideas, trigger fear of taking a wrong step in a high-stakes situation, or unleash frenetic but ineffective activity.

Somewhere in between these two extremes is the ideal level of stress—one that creates positive pressure in the direction of change without causing debilitating worry. This magic zone is what John Kotter referred to as the "productive range of distress." This is an extremely useful concept for managers who are leading through change, but how do you take it from being conceptual to being real? How can you alter the levels of stress on your team? How do you know when you should intervene?

Your first step is to assess the current state. There are signs that the stress levels on your team aren't sufficient to create meaningful change. Watch for people who are too comfortable with the status quo—either resisting the need to change, referring incessantly to the "way we used to do it," or generally not applying themselves to get the job done (such as coming in late, taking long breaks, and yabba dabba doo-ing like Fred Flintstone at the end-of-day whistle).

The bigger challenge is to identify the people who are burdened by too much stress. It's tricky because some people will have an obvious, frenetic, or panicked stress response, whereas others will withdraw and direct their stress inward. Because there is no single pattern, you're looking for deviations from an employee's normal behavior. Is someone working considerably longer hours, failing to take breaks or to get lunch, behaving irritably with coworkers? On the other end of the spectrum, is someone becoming disturbingly quiet? Are they interacting with you noticeably less frequently? Is their body language demonstrating fatigue or cause for concern? Those changes might suggest too much stress. Another option is to ask people how they're feeling, as Allison Rimm recommends in chapter 3.

Once you have a sense of the stress levels on your team, you'll know whether you need to dial the heat up or bring it back down from a boil to a simmer. There are several techniques you can use for each scenario.

If you believe there is too little stress on your team and that it will take a little more discomfort before your employees are in the productive range of distress, you have a variety of options to choose from. To make the suggestions concrete, I'm going to use the example of the introduction of a new sales culture. This is a common transformation and one that will stall with too little heat and blow up with too much.

Increase the frequency and pointedness of coaching

It's easy to stick to the status quo when no one is watching. The moment that an employee knows that you're noticing her behavior, the stress levels will naturally rise. The secret to coaching toward an optimal level of stress is to increase the frequency of the feedback you provide, but decrease the intensity. Imagine you have rolled out new sales management software, but you're struggling to get all of the salespeople to record their activity. Try simple feedback such as, "It's Wednesday and I'm only seeing three opportunities in the funnel for this week." Pair the feedback with a question such as, "What time of day works best for you to input your meetings?"

If you don't see improvement, dial it up: "I've made three requests for people to input and I've only seen two new entries. This has become a problem. I'd like each of you to come to me today and share how you're going to change your routine to include your responsibilities for tracking sales activity daily."

Connect the person's behavior to something bigger and more important

Sometimes an employee hasn't made the link between how they perform and the organization's ability to achieve something critical. The salesperson who is consistently delinquent in entering opportunities needs to know that big decisions are made using real-time pipeline data. Pricing, products, and promotions might all be affected by a pipeline that appears tepid, when in fact there are just opportunities missing. Help your team understand the trickle-down effects by saying something like: "I had to go into the regional leadership team meeting today with a pipeline that shows only about 30% of what it should show. The VP was alarmed and started talking about a few drastic actions. I had to assure him that the data isn't representative, but I won't get away with that again."

Allow a natural negative consequence for a lack of action

Often, as a manager, you're so invested in the performance of your team that you're willing to pick up the slack from poor performance to avoid a bad outcome. That only reinforces the employees' perceptions that they don't need to change. Instead, allow poor performance to lead to a natural consequence.

In the sales example, if you ask the regional VP not to discuss any opportunities that are not in the system, your technology holdouts will be left out of the discussion. Salespeople are fueled by posting wins, and this loss of recognition might just spur some action. Given that the missing pipeline numbers will also reflect poorly on you and your whole team, you have the added benefit of a little peer pressure to get them on board.

Knowing how to turn up the heat is valuable, but sometimes you have the opposite problem. When the pressure mounts, you might need to do one of the following to settle things down:

Provide frequent positive feedback

In the low-stress scenario, you were coaching frequently to increase the sense of accountability. In the high-stress situation, you should still be spending considerable time coaching and providing feedback, but you need to change the content and tone. Your content should be focused more on recognizing and reinforcing small victories and on helping to problem-solve to create momentum. Your tone should be calm and reassuring. You want your team to feel that they're making headway. In the sales example, you can pivot a conversation about a new prospect to "Hey, let's enter that into the system together now."

Break the problem into smaller pieces

Our language is full of metaphors for the sense of overwhelm we get when we try to tackle something too large. Whether they're swallowing elephants or boiling oceans, your employees are signaling that they're shutting down because of the magnitude of the challenge. At that point (or hopefully before), help each person zoom in on a specific part of the project. You can divide the project among a group of people so each person has a manageable chunk.

You can also break the project into sequential steps and focus on one at a time. The goal is to make the next task seem surmountable. You're not climbing Everest; you're just getting to base camp. "This week, we're going to focus on the automotive sector. Let's get all of our automotive leads into the system."

Add structure to the problem

One of the worst things you can do when stress levels get too high is to jump in and solve the problem for your team. That can send all the wrong messages and leave you with accountability issues over the long run. The alternative is to go a little further than normal in helping your team think about how to tackle the problem.

Many people get stressed in the face of too much complexity. If you can give them a path, they can wrap their heads around it. For example, you could say, "First solve for how you're going to roll out the new pricing, then you can go back and apply that to direct sales. Don't even worry about the indirect channel until later."

Model confidence

Whether you believe the hype about mirror neurons or not, you know from experience that emotions in the office can be contagious. The simplest way you can turn down the heat for your team is to show them with your words and your body language that you believe everything will work out. If you're running around like a chicken with its head cut off, you'll incite panic in everyone else. If you are calm, deliberate, and decisive, you'll help keep employees' stress levels from getting too high.

In some cases, the stress levels of your team members will be uniformly high or low. That allows you to use one common approach for everyone. Unfortunately, it's more likely that different people will be in very different head spaces; some thriving on the heat of the moment and others shriveling in it. When different team members are experiencing the stress of the change differently, you'll need to have more targeted one-on-one conversations that give you the opportunity to adjust the heat. If you're accustomed to huddling your team and sharing direction with everyone at once, this might require a temporary shift in approach.

Regardless of whether the heat needs to go up or down, your job is to monitor constantly and to make the course corrections that will keep your team in the productive range of distress. That's the magic zone where change happens.

———————

Liane Davey is the cofounder of 3COze Inc. She is the author of *You First: Inspire Your Team to Grow Up, Get Along, and Get Stuff Done* and a coauthor of *Leadership Solutions: The Pathway to Bridge the Leadership Gap.* Follow her on Twitter @LianeDavey.

CHAPTER 23

Burnout at Work Isn't Just About Exhaustion. It's Also About Loneliness

By Emma Seppala and Marissa King

More and more people are feeling tired and lonely at work. In analyzing the General Social Survey of 2016, we found that, compared with roughly 20 years ago, people are twice as likely to report that they are always exhausted. Close to 50% of people say they are often or

Adapted from content posted on hbr.org, June 29, 2017 (product #H03R71).

always exhausted due to work. This is a shockingly high statistic—and it's a 32% increase from two decades ago. What's more, there is a significant correlation between work exhaustion and feeling lonely: The more people are exhausted, the lonelier they feel.

This loneliness is not a result of social isolation, as you might think, but rather is due to the emotional exhaustion of workplace burnout. In researching the book *The Happiness Track*, we found that 50% of people—across professions, from the nonprofit sector to the medical field—are burned out. This isn't just a problem for busy, overworked executives (though the high rates of loneliness and burnout among this group are well known). Our work suggests that the problem is pervasive across professions and up and down corporate hierarchies.

Loneliness, whether it results from social isolation or exhaustion, has serious consequences for individuals. John Cacioppo, a leading expert on loneliness and coauthor of *Loneliness: Human Nature and the Need for Social Connection*, emphasizes its tremendous impact on psychological and physical health and longevity. Research by Sarah Pressman, of the University of California, Irvine, corroborates his work and demonstrates that while obesity reduces longevity by 20%, drinking by 30%, and smoking by 50%, loneliness reduces it by a whopping 70%. In fact, one study by Nicole Valtorta and colleagues suggests that loneliness increases your chance of stroke or coronary heart disease—the leading cause of death in developed countries—by 30%.[1] On the other hand, feelings of social connection can strengthen our immune system, lengthen our life, and lower rates of anxiety and depression.

As anyone who has experienced it can attest, loneliness is an emotionally painful feeling; it even registers as physical pain in the brain, according to a Carnegie Mellon University study.[2] The social repercussions of this discomfort directly impact work productivity because people disengage. And both the Smith School of Business at Queen's University's Best Small and Medium Employers in Canada study and the Gallup organization's State of the American Workplace report have shown the extreme costs to companies of disengagement: almost 37% higher absenteeism, 49% more accidents, 16% lower profitability, and a 65% lower share price over time.

In the meantime, experts and companies have struggled to figure out how to counter growing levels of burnout. Many recommendations focus on relieving stress, teaching mindfulness, or reducing workload—all of which treat burnout as an individual condition. But its link to loneliness suggests that greater human connection at work may also be key to solving the burnout problem.

In fact, research has demonstrated the link between social support at work, lower rates of burnout, and greater work satisfaction and productivity. For example, the most important factor in work happiness, one study commissioned by the Association of Accounting Technicians in the United Kingdom showed, is positive social relationships with coworkers. Workplace engagement is associated with positive social relations that involve feeling valued, supported, respected, and secure. And the result of feeling socially connected, studies show, is greater psychological well-being, which translates into higher productivity and performance. This is true in part because social connectedness leads to higher self-esteem, which means employees are more trusting, empathic, and cooperative—leading others to trust and cooperate with them.

So what can leaders and employees do?

Promote a workplace culture of inclusion and empathy

Research by the University of Michigan's Kim Cameron, author of *Positive Leadership*, shows that workplaces characterized by caring, supportive, respectful, honest, and forgiving relationships lead to higher organizational performance overall. You want to encourage community and value warm, friendly, and understanding relationships between people. Empathy, in particular, may be a protective factor against burnout and work exhaustion, studies suggest. Jane Dutton, professor at the University of Michigan and coauthor of *Awakening Compassion at Work*, persuasively argues that compassion can foster greater workplace resilience overall.

Encourage employees throughout the organization to build developmental networks

These networks are small groups of colleagues you routinely turn to for task advice or emotional support. At the vast majority of companies, creation of these networks is left up to chance. However, companies and managers can help foster them by assigning onboarding partners and helping employees access and connect with potential mentors, coaches, and peers. Removing barriers to connect, by freeing space in calendars and offering contact information with relevant background information (including hobbies and interests, not just work), can go a long way.

Celebrate collective successes

The happiness arising from a happy hour is short-lived. But celebrating collective successes helps create a sense of belonging and attachment in organizations. One of the best examples we have seen of this was at Awethu Project, a startup incubator in South Africa. Each time a new employee was hired into a venture, a bell rang, and everyone stopped what they were doing to cheer. This kind of ritual builds solidarity, increases a sense of belonging, and can help guard against burnout.

The stakes for companies are high when it comes to loneliness and burnout. A recent report from the New Economics Foundation estimates that loneliness costs employers in the United Kingdom billions of dollars each year. And according to the APA's Stress in America report, employee burnout costs the U.S. healthcare system hundreds of billions of dollars each year. The research is clear. Now it's time for managers and leaders to take steps to battle these epidemics.

———————

Emma Seppala, PhD, is the science director of Stanford University's Center for Compassion and Altruism Research and Education and author of *The Happiness Track*. She is also founder of Fulfillment Daily. Follow her on Twitter @emmaseppala or her website www .emmaseppala.com. **Marissa King, PhD,** is professor of organizational behavior at the Yale School of Management. Her research and teaching examine social networks, well-being, and work.

NOTES

1. N. K. Valtorta, M. Kanaan, S. Gilbody, et al, "Loneliness and Social Isolation as Risk Factors for Coronary Heart Disease and Stroke: Systematic Review and Meta-analysis of Longitudinal Observational Studies," *Heart* 102, no. 13 (2016): 1009–1016.

2. N. I. Eisenberger, M. D. Lieberman, and K. D. Williams, "Does Rejection Hurt? An FMRI Study of Social Exclusion," *Science* 302, no. 10 (2003), 290–292.

CHAPTER 24

Don't Let Grunt Work Drag Down Performance

by Whitney Johnson

In *So I Married an Axe Murderer*, a wacky 1990s parody, a police officer named Tony confides to his captain, "I'm having doubts about being a cop. You know, it's not like how it is on TV. All I do all day is fill out forms and paperwork."

Tony thought his job would be more thrilling than it has turned out to be. Tony is not alone. Every job contains some unglamorous grunt work.

I am a great proponent of the joys of work. But not every part of every job is a joy. While we all want to find

Adapted from "How to Help Your Team Manage Grunt Work" on hbr.org, September 20, 2018 (product #H04JNH).

a level of meaning and purpose in our work, often some fraction of our time has to be spent doing tasks that have no intrinsic meaning and serve no deeper purpose than helping to keep the trains running.

This can be especially tough for early-career professionals to accept, especially those in entry-level positions. College life is often flexible, challenging, and engaging, and after four years of that it can be hard to sit still in an office for hours at time, doing administrative tasks, without thinking, *I earned a college degree for this?* But it's not just recent graduates who struggle with grunt work. Anyone of any age can think their role should entail only tasks that are exciting or fulfilling and that the drudge work is beneath them and should be someone else's problem.

Whatever its source, entitlement is a career killer, a noose with which employees of any generation can—and do—hang themselves. If someone you manage is complaining to you about the amount of grunt work they have, you need to figure out a way to help them get over their frustration and see that everyone on the team has grunt work they have to do, and also learn to manage their time so that they don't shortchange higher-value activities. (For the purposes of this article, I'm assuming that as a manager, you've assigned these tasks fairly, and the employee in question isn't actually burdened with too many non-promotable tasks.)

Here are a few techniques I suggest to help people shrink the amount of time they spend on grunt work, while still getting it done:

Impose constraints

If an employee is filling her days with low-level tasks that could be completed in much less time, impose a time constraint. Morning email needs to be answered by 10 a.m. Calls need to be returned within one hour. The previous week's data needs to be compiled and reported by Monday at 4 p.m.

Time management is a skill that many need help to learn, and as a manager, you may need to be the teacher. Expect some pushback—an employee is likely to say that they can't complete X task in half the time. But push them to at least try. They may surprise themselves. And an often-overlooked upside is that a ho-hum task can become a more engaging challenge when a time constraint is imposed.

Dangle the carrot

What is the more interesting work that the employee would like to be doing? What is your vision of what the employee could be doing for the firm? Have the conversation. Help the employee visualize the new opportunities that could complement their ordinary tasks. Perhaps pair the employee with a more mature worker who can mentor them in time management and also inspire with a glimpse of the different types of work the firm engages in. Adding more-appealing work to their portfolio will compel them to shrink the amount of time they spend on lower-value work.

Shake the stick

A dangled carrot is positive motivation, but consequences can be effective as well. Employees who spend hours on tasks that really are not that important are not spending their time on the right things. Establish goals for an employee's most value-added work, and consequences if they don't meet those goals.

Shrinking the amount of time your employee is spending on the dull tasks should help mitigate their frustration at having to do them at all. If it doesn't, you may need to have a larger conversation about their career goals and whether they can meet them in their current role, or even at your firm.

Remind them that positivity itself is promotable

When you hire or promote someone, it's because of what you think they can do for your organization. But you also want to hire people who have a good attitude—who will pitch in and do what needs to be done. Sometimes taking care of the grunt work is just about showing that you can be a team player with a great attitude. If a manager can trust you with the boring stuff, then you can definitely be trusted with the exciting stuff. Remind your employee that sometimes, it's not about *what* you're doing but *how* you go about doing it.

Model the behavior

So much work is invisible. We know what we're spending time on, but does anyone else? When an employee complains about the scut work they have to do, it's probably because they don't see how much scut work everyone—including their boss—has to do. Make the work on your team more transparent. Talk to the employee about how everyone—even you—has to spend a certain percentage of their time on these kinds of tasks. Make sure your team sees that you are occasionally in the same boat.

I love the story told about Sam Pitroda, then the head of C-DOT, India's telecommunications enterprise. C-DOT had two floors of a five-star hotel as their workspace. A repairman had been called to fix a broken doorknob in the boardroom. Repair completed, he packed up his tools and prepared to leave—both the boardroom and the mess he'd made while making the repair. Pitroda asked for a broom, invited the man to sit, and proceeded to clean up the mess while he watched. A great lesson, which should be taught in more workplaces—the task is not beneath the CEO; it isn't beneath anyone else either.

Whitney Johnson is an executive coach, speaker, and innovation thinker recently named one of the most influential management thinkers by Thinkers50. She is the author of *Build an A-Team* from Harvard Business Review Press and the critically acclaimed *Disrupt Yourself.*

Create a Culture of Engagement

CHAPTER 25

Positive Work Cultures Are More Productive

by Emma Seppala and Kim Cameron

Too many companies bet on having a cutthroat, high-pressure, take-no-prisoners culture to drive their financial success.

But a large and growing body of research on positive organizational psychology demonstrates that not only is a cutthroat environment harmful to productivity over time, but that a positive environment will lead to dramatic benefits for employers, employees, and the bottom line.

Adapted from "Proof That Positive Work Cultures Are More Productive" on hbr.org, December 1, 2015 (product #H02IMC).

Although there's an assumption that stress and pressure push employees to perform more, better, and faster, what cutthroat organizations fail to recognize is the hidden costs incurred.

First, research by Sunday Azagba and Mesbah Sharaf shows that healthcare expenditures at high-pressure companies are nearly 50% greater than at other organizations.[1] As noted in chapter 23, workplace stress costs the U.S. economy billions of dollars, plus 550 million workdays each year. Stress is responsible for 60–80% of workplace accidents, and, according to the American Institute of Stress, more than 80% of doctor visits. Workplace stress has been linked to health problems ranging from metabolic syndrome to cardiovascular disease and mortality.

Second is the cost of disengagement. While a cutthroat environment and a culture of fear can motivate (and sometimes even excite) for a time, research suggests that the inevitable stress it creates will likely lead to disengagement over the long term. And, as we know from the data covered in this book, disengagement is costly: It affects absenteeism, safety, quality of work, productivity, and profitability, among other things.

Lack of loyalty is a third cost. Research, again, from the American Stress Institute, shows that workplace stress leads to an increase of almost 50% in voluntary turnover. People go on the job market, decline promotions, or resign. And the turnover costs associated with recruiting, training, reduced productivity, lost expertise, and so forth, are significant. The Center for American Progress estimates that replacing a single employee costs approximately 20% of that employee's salary.[2]

Many companies throw perks at the problem. However, a Gallup poll showed that, even when workplaces offered benefits such as flextime and work-from-home opportunities, engagement predicted well-being above and beyond anything else.[3] When surveyed by the Association of Accounting Technicians, employees preferred being happy at work (which included factors such as working with good people, enjoying the role, and getting along with the boss) to material benefits.

Well-being comes from one place, and one place only—a positive culture.

As this book suggests, managers play a critical role in shaping people's daily experience of work. In her introduction, Susan David notes that the best place to start when it comes to motivation is at the team level. Actions taken here to improve the conditions for engagement—for people opting to bring their best selves to work—can multiply and spread through the rest of the organization. Creating a healthy culture for your team rests on a few major principles. Our own research has found that a positive workplace culture boils down to six essential characteristics, all of which can be supported or stifled by direct supervisors:

- Caring for, being interested in, and maintaining responsibility for colleagues as friends

- Providing support for one another, including offering kindness and compassion when others are struggling

- Avoiding blame and forgiving mistakes

- Inspiring one another at work

- Emphasizing the meaningfulness of the work (as described in section 3)

- Treating one another with respect, gratitude, trust, and integrity

As a boss, how can you foster these qualities on your team? The research points to four steps to try:

1. **Foster social connections.** A large number of empirical studies confirm that positive social connections at work produce highly desirable results. For example, people get sick less often, recover twice as fast from surgery, experience less depression, learn faster and remember longer, tolerate pain and discomfort better, display more mental acuity, and perform better on the job. Conversely, research by Sarah Pressman, described in chapter 23, found that the probability of dying early is 70% higher for people with poor social relationships. Toxic, stress-filled workplaces affect social relationships and, consequently, life expectancy.

2. **Show empathy.** As a boss, you have a huge impact on how your employees feel. A telling brain-imaging study by Richard Boyatzis and others found that, when employees recalled a boss that had been unkind or un-empathic, they showed increased activation in areas of the brain associated with avoidance and negative emotion while the opposite was true when they recalled

an empathic boss. Moreover, Jane Dutton and her colleagues in the CompassionLab at the University of Michigan suggest that leaders who demonstrate compassion toward employees foster individual and collective resilience in challenging times.

3. **Go out of your way to help.** Ever had a manager or mentor who took a lot of trouble to help you when he or she didn't have to? Chances are you have remained loyal to that person to this day. Jonathan Haidt at New York University's Stern School of Business shows in his research that when leaders are not just fair but self-sacrificing, their employees are actually moved and inspired to become more loyal and committed themselves. As a consequence, they are more likely to go out of their way to be helpful and friendly to other employees, thus creating a self-reinforcing cycle. Daan Van Knippenberg of Rotterdam School of Management shows that employees of self-sacrificing leaders are more cooperative because they trust their leaders more. They are also more productive and see their leaders as more effective and charismatic.

4. **Encourage people to talk to you—especially about their problems.** Not surprisingly, trusting that a leader has your best interests at heart improves employee performance. Employees feel safe rather than fearful and, as research by Amy Edmondson of Harvard demonstrates in her

work on psychological safety, a culture of safety, in which leaders are inclusive, humble, and encourage their staff to speak up or ask for help, leads to better learning and performance outcomes. Rather than creating a culture of fear of negative consequences, ensuring people feel safe in the workplace helps encourage the spirit of experimentation so critical for innovation. Kamal Birdi of Sheffield University has shown that empowerment, when coupled with good training and teamwork, leads to superior performance outcomes whereas a range of efficient manufacturing and operations practices do not.

When you know a leader is committed to operating from a set of values based on interpersonal kindness, he or she sets the tone for the entire organization. In *Give and Take*, Wharton professor Adam Grant demonstrates that leader kindness and generosity are strong predictors of team and organizational effectiveness. Whereas harsh work climates are linked to poorer employee health, the opposite is true of positive work climates where employees tend to have lower heart rates and blood pressure as well as stronger immune systems. A positive work climate leads to a positive workplace culture, which, again, boosts commitment, engagement, and performance.

In sum, a positive workplace is more successful over time because it increases positive emotions and well-being. This, in turn, improves people's relationships with each other and amplifies their abilities and their creativity. It buffers against negative experiences such as stress, thus improving employees' ability to bounce back from challenges and difficulties while bolstering their health. And, it attracts employees, making them more loyal to the leader and to the organization as well as bringing out their best strengths. When organizations and managers work to develop positive, virtuous cultures they achieve significantly higher levels of organizational effectiveness—including financial performance, customer satisfaction, productivity, and employee engagement.

———————

Emma Seppala, PhD, is the science director of Stanford University's Center for Compassion and Altruism Research and Education and author of *The Happiness Track*. She is also founder of Fulfillment Daily. Follow her on Twitter @emmaseppala or her website www .emmaseppala.com. **Kim Cameron, PhD,** is the William Russell Kelly Professor of Management and Organizations at the Ross School of Business at the University of Michigan and the author of *Positive Leadership* and *Practicing Positive Leadership*.

NOTES

1. S. Azagba and M. Sharaf, "Psychosocial Working Conditions and the Utilization of Health Care Services," *BMC Public Health* 11 (2011): 642.

2. Heather Boushey and Sarah Jane Glynn, "There Are Significant Business Costs to Replacing Employees," Center for American Progress, November 12, 2012, https://www.americanprogress.org/issues/ economy/reports/2012/11/16/44464/there-are-significant-business -costs-to-replacing-employees/.

3. Teresa Tritch, "Engagement Drives Results at New Century," *Gallup Management Journal*, September 11, 2003, https://www.nova .edu/ie/ice/forms/engagement_drives_results.pdf.

CHAPTER 26

Flex Work Doesn't Help Employees If It Hurts Their Careers

by Lindsey Trimble O'Connor and Erin Cech

When you think about who needs flexibility at work to manage personal and family responsibilities, who comes to mind? If you are like most people, you envision a working mom.

The prevailing assumption is that working mothers are the ones who want and need flexibility at work. To be sure, many working mothers still shoulder the daunting double shift of full-time work and primary child

Adapted from "Your Flex Work Culture Doesn't Help Employees If It Hurts Their Careers" on hbr.org, June 12, 2018 (product #H04DOE).

care responsibilities, and many likely want jobs that give them more flexibility to juggle these important responsibilities. Nearly two decades of research shows that working flexibly is akin to a career torpedo for many working moms: Those who do it are often "mommy-tracked" into less demanding, lower-paying positions, and in the worst-case scenarios, they're pushed out of their jobs entirely.

But we suspected that flexibility is not just a "woman's issue." Everyone needs flexibility at some point in their careers, whether to take a pet to the veterinarian, to serve as the best man in a brother's wedding, or to pay last respects at a great aunt's funeral. And working moms may not be the only ones who suffer professionally and personally when they feel unable to negotiate their work around the stuff of real life. So we asked a question that's rarely been addressed in academic studies: What happens to all employees when they feel that working flexibly at their organization will derail their careers?

In two studies, recently published in *Sociological Perspectives* and *Community, Work, & Family*, we examined how workplace flexibility bias—employees' belief that people at their workplace are unlikely to get ahead if they take leave or work flexibly—affects people's engagement at work, their intentions to stay or leave their jobs, their ability to balance their work and personal lives, and even their health.[1]

Our data comes from a nationally representative sample of about 2,700 U.S. employees collected by the Families & Work Institute. In the survey, employees were asked about the extent to which others at their workplace were likely to get ahead at work if they took time off or rearranged their schedules for family or personal reasons. Our analysis includes employees from a range of occupations, industries, and sectors and from different racial, ethnic, and socioeconomic backgrounds. Thus, we were able to account for a variety of factors that might affect employees' attitudes toward their jobs, their experiences with work-life spillover, and their health.

We show that when employees see workplace flexibility bias in their organizations, they are less happy professionally and are more likely to say they will quit their jobs in the near future. Importantly, the effects of this bias aren't limited to working mothers. Even men who don't have kids and who have never taken family leave or worked flexibly are harmed when they see flexibility bias in their workplaces.

We also find that perceiving bias against people who work flexibly not only impacts work attitudes but also follows employees home. It increases their experiences with work-life spillover, minor health problems, and depressive symptoms, as well as leading to more absenteeism at work and worse self-rated health and sleep. These effects occur for working moms, dads, and childless women and men alike. The effect holds across age groups and racial and ethnic categories as well.

Why is workplace flexibility bias so harmful to all types of employees? We think employees generally do not like working for organizations that penalize people for having lives outside of work. They don't feel supported, and they feel a lack of control over their schedules. We also speculate that flexibility bias limits the extent to which employees can attend to their personal and family responsibilities, and does so in ways that are harmful to their health (for example, when someone puts off going to the doctor because she is afraid to take time away from work).

We are not suggesting that employees have no responsibility to show up consistently and be engaged. Worker absenteeism and disengagement are undoubtedly multi-billion-dollar problems in the United States. However, when organizations ignore employees' personal and family lives—and harbor workplace cultures that leave them afraid to ask for or use the leave and flexibility they need—organizations are likely exacerbating these problems, not solving them.

Our research also shows that having an engaged, committed, and healthy workforce does not come just from offering a generous suite of family leave and flexible work options. Organizations also need to pay close attention to the messages they send to employees about actually using these policies. A great set of flexible policies from HR means little when employees think their careers will be derailed by them.

In order to understand whether this feeling is prevalent in your organization, start by looking into how frequently your flexibility options are being used, and by whom. Previous research by Mary Blair-Loy and Amy Wharton shows workers often avoid taking leave or working flexibly even when they need to, out of the fear of what it will do to their careers. If employees, or some subgroups of employees, are not taking advantage of flexible work options when they need them, that is a red flag.

THREE WAYS TO MAKE YOUR WORKPLACE MORE FLEXIBILITY-FRIENDLY

by Nathaniel Koloc

1. Ask your employees which kinds of flexibility they want, and be prepared to act on their requests

Depending on your industry, the product or service that you sell, and your geographic location, your employees' needs will vary. And it's impossible to know what they want unless you ask them. Employers have many options when it comes to increasing freedom: remote work, work-from-home, and paid vacation policies are some of the more commonly known. But you can also let employees choose their work and managers, select their own professional development opportunities, or provide incentive-based compensation for particularly good performance on key projects.

In-person facilitated discussions—not faceless surveys—are the best way to hear from people as they are more likely to give you authentic responses. Work-life balance is a very personal thing and to get the full picture it's important to listen carefully. If your organization is too large to hear from everyone in person, make sure to at least flesh out survey results with a few facilitated discussions from different functional teams.

2. Spend time understanding remote communication tools

Companies like Slack, Hipchat, Yammer, Trello, and Asana are bringing fantastic tools to the marketplace

(continued)

THREE WAYS TO MAKE YOUR WORKPLACE MORE FLEXIBILITY-FRIENDLY

that make it easier than ever before for remote team members to communicate and work together, as well as interact with company stakeholders. (I think that Slack is especially fantastic.) Professionals who use Twitter and other social networks for professional reasons are always a tweet away from their teams.

If you're not sure what team communication tools to use, get in touch with either a startup founder or folks who work in your local startup ecosystem. They are more likely to know of the latest offering that has been faring well with early adopters.

3. Be vocal about your work policies related to flexibility

Adopting high-freedom policies is a competitive advantage in the talent market. The more nuanced and relevant your policies are, the more competitive your hiring brand will be. If you have great benefits but don't have a dedicated (and concise) section of your

If employees at your organization are scared to take leave or work flexibly, there are things you can do. For one, senior management can lead by example. When managers take full paternity and maternity leaves, head home early a few days a week to help their children off the school bus, or arrive late after a dentist appointment, those around them feel less anxiety about taking leave or working flexibly. (For other suggestions, see the sidebar,

careers page or job descriptions that explains them, or you don't talk about them during candidate interviews, you're missing an opportunity to leverage that asset.

It's much easier to recruit and retain great talent when you are giving employees what they want while helping them excel at their jobs. More and more people want the freedom to decide where, when, how, and with whom they work. Do your best to provide that freedom.

Nathaniel Koloc is cofounder and CEO of ReWork, a mission-driven recruiting company that specializes in sourcing purpose-driven professionals for companies operating in the purpose economy.

Excerpted from "Let Employees Choose When, Where, and How They Work" on hbr.org, November 10, 2014 (product #H012C7).

"Three Ways to Make Your Workplace More Flexibility-Friendly.") Organizations that take these steps will likely find their employees healthier, more productive, and more committed.

Lindsey Trimble O'Connor is an assistant professor of sociology at California State University who studies the social psychological, organizational, and cultural forces perpetuating workplace inequalities against women and workers with caregiving responsibilities. **Erin Cech** is an assistant professor of sociology at the University of Michigan. She studies cultural processes of inequality reproduction, particularly through the mechanisms of the "passion principle," the meritocratic ideology, and popular definitions of good work and good workers.

NOTE

1. Lindsey Trimble O'Connor and Erin A. Cech, "Not Just a Mothers' Problem: The Consequences of Perceived Workplace Flexibility Bias for All Workers," *Sociological Perspectives* 61, no. 5 (2018): 808–829; and Erin A. Cech and Lindsey Trimble O'Connor, "'Like Second-Hand Smoke': The Toxic Effect of Workplace Flexibility Bias for Workers' Health," *Community, Work & Family* 20, no. 5 (2017) 543–572.

CHAPTER 27

Rules for Designing an Inspiring Workplace

by Sally Augustin

Good design has a powerful influence on how people think and behave. As today's companies wake up to the value of workers who are truly engaged in their work—a clear case of trying to encourage certain ways of thinking and behaving—they should probably be paying far more attention to *place design*. Few things are more instrumental in boosting—or diminishing—levels of employee engagement.

Adapted from "Rules for Designing an Engaging Workplace" on hbr .org, October 28, 2014 (product #H011E5).

Environmental psychologists are the design mavens of the scientific world. We're the folks who examine how sensory experiences, psychosocial factors such as needing a territory, and basic psychological drives like having control over our physical environment, interact with personality and national culture to influence how we respond to and are affected by different spaces.

One of the things that environmental psychologists look at is how design affects mood. Through psychological chain reactions, mood influences engagement; more positive moods are linked to higher levels of engagement. Designing for engagement, therefore, means designing spaces that make positive moods more likely.

While many organizations rely on mission and vision statements to convey how prized employees are by the people issuing their paychecks, there are few things more powerful than spending money (and time and thought) on designing a workplace that *shows* people the value of their well-being and productivity and supports them as they do their jobs every day.

But workplace design isn't always effective. Generally, designers talk to employees who will work in a space about their jobs and how the space can optimize their performance. Often, the end result doesn't align with those conversations. A workplace gets designed to look good (like the one the CEO saw in a glossy magazine spread), or like it may accomplish some ill-defined objective, such as increasing collaboration. (For surprising evidence of what many employees *do* want in a workspace, see the sidebar "The Number One Office Perk Is Not What You Think.")

THE NUMBER ONE OFFICE PERK
IS NOT WHAT YOU THINK

by Jean C. Meister

The news headlines about what perks or elements of office design make for a great employee experience seem to be dominated by fads—think treadmill desks, nap pods, and "bring your dog to work day."

However, a new survey by the HR advisory firm Future Workplace called "The Employee Experience" reveals that, in reality, employees crave something far more fundamental and essential to human needs. In a poll of 1,614 North American employees, we found that *access to natural light* and *views of the outdoors* are the number one attribute of the workplace environment, outranking stalwarts like onsite cafeterias and fitness centers, and premium perks including on-site childcare.

The study also found that the absence of natural light and outdoor views hurts the employee experience. Over a third of employees feel that they don't get enough natural light in their workspace. In fact, 47% of employees admit they feel tired or very tired from the absence of natural light or a window at their office, and 43% report feeling gloomy because of the lack of light.

Research by Cornell professor Alan Hedge found that optimization of natural light in an office significantly improves health and wellness among workers.

(continued)

THE NUMBER ONE OFFICE PERK IS NOT WHAT YOU THINK

In fact, this study revealed that workers in daylight office environments reported a 51% drop in the incidence of eyestrain, a 63% drop in the incidence of headaches, and a 56% reduction in drowsiness.

What can managers do to increase employees' exposure to natural light? Emma Seppala and Johann Berlin suggest providing spaces for taking lunch and breaks outdoors and encouraging people to schedule walking meetings outside. Make sure window blinds are open wherever possible, and if people can't get outside, bring the outdoors in with indoor gardens, green walls, plants (as many as possible) around the office, or even nature photography, artwork, or video. These small steps could significantly boost employees' moods.

———

Jeanne C. Meister is partner at Future Workplace, an HR advisory and research firm and the coauthor of two books on the future of work: *The 2020 Workplace* and *The Future Workplace Experience.*

Adapted from "The Number One Office Perk? Natural Light" on hbr.org, September 3, 2018 (product #H04IT7) and "Why You Should Tell Your Team to Take a Break and Go Outside" on hbr.org, June 26, 2017 (product #H03QWZ).

Workspaces should be designed so that each worker can add the most value to their employer's bottom line, regardless of their role. Most workers need to be able to concentrate on the task at hand, and that's difficult in a field of cubicles or in a sea of faces when the cubicles are removed and everyone is asked to sit at long tables. And despite popular belief, those open spaces aren't spurring useful communication. Research consistently shows that constructive, work-related collaboration doesn't increase when work environments are made more open.

Some companies try to get around the pitfalls of open offices by providing a range of different workspaces. While a smorgasbord of options is better than asking people to work in chaos, it's insufficient. Research also shows that people lose concentration every time they are interrupted, including when they have to pack up and move to a quieter place in the office.

So where does that leave us when designing an engaging workplace? Here are a few ideas:

Don't underestimate the power of color. When people are doing work that requires deep thinking and concentration, the places where they're working should be relaxing. When the work is less mentally taxing, more energizing spaces are fine. We're relaxed in the presence of colors that aren't very saturated but are relatively bright and that aren't cluttered. Moderate visual complexity is best. That means the space should include only a few colors and patterns, and that decorative objects should be carefully curated, for example. Stark colors should be avoided; they're alien to the environments in which we developed as a species and make us tense.

Get outsiders to ask questions. Workers interpret their environments based on their national culture, organizational culture, professional culture (associated with their function, like engineer or accountant) and personal experiences. But they can also be hesitant to speak candidly when face-to-face with their boss. Want to know what your employees think about their workspace? Get someone from outside the firm to ask them, guarantee that all responses will be anonymous and kept confidential, and listen.

Let your workers have some of the control. Workplaces that support engagement communicate that employees are valued and also give workers some control over the physical experiences they have at the office. Let your employees have some input into lighting (even if it's just providing desk lamps) and temperature settings. Incorporate some spaces where furnishings can be reconfigured on the fly, at least to some extent, and others where people can have privacy when they need it. In many workplaces today, employees can only find visual and acoustic privacy in the bathroom. All humans need privacy sometimes, whether it's to focus on a task, collect our thoughts, or take a call from our child's school.

Consider the chipmunk test. When you're thinking about furnishings and architectural features in workplaces, keep chipmunks in mind. Humans are comfortable in the sorts of protected seats with a view over the surrounding area that give us the same secure feeling a chipmunk would have, snuggled in a comfy nest in tree branches. Similar spaces are easy to introduce into modern workplaces. Tuck small meeting areas into alcoves off hallways or larger workspaces. You get bonus points if these spaces are raised a step and a tiny bit darker than the surrounding area. Next time you see seats lined up with their backs to an aisle or walkway, ask yourself, would a chipmunk want to sit with his back exposed like that? Is this positioning natural? Would chipmunks—or humans—feel vulnerable or at ease here?

Workplace design can be a powerful force for enhancing—or detracting from—employee engagement. Honest design, spaces that reflect employees' needs and concerns (a subset of which are presented here), is something that employees notice, interpret, and value.

———————

Sally Augustin is a practicing design/environmental psychologist, an expert on person-centered design, and a principal at Design with Science. She consults with organizations and individuals to inform optimal design solutions.

CHAPTER 28

IDEO's Engagement Formula

by Duane Bray

This volume covers a lot of great research on and advice about how to motivate people to do their best work. With so many possible mechanisms, how do you choose the right ones and piece them together to create a true culture of engagement? This chapter brings the focus in to one company—IDEO—and to the particular recipe that's worked for us. This engagement formula has been key to our success and our reputation as an innovation leader. It's part of the DNA of our company, there from the start and still present in everything we do.

Adapted from "IDEO's Employee Engagement Formula" on hbr.org, December 18, 2015 (product #H02KH5).

IDEO's origin story sometimes sounds like a myth or a fable, but it's actually true. David Kelley founded the company with a simple goal: to create a workplace made up of his best friends. In the beginning he did, in fact, bring in some of his closest buddies to launch the Silicon Valley firm that would become IDEO. More than 30 years later, we're a global design company that employs more than 650 people. Obviously, we didn't get to that size by hiring only our friends. But David's early intention still greatly informs the way we work. There are, in fact, four elements of our culture that came directly from his founding statement. We think they're essential factors in keeping employees engaged—not just at our company but at any company.

Permission to Play

When people play together, they form stronger bonds and are more willing to take risks and imagine new possibilities with one another. Employees need to know that experimentation is not only allowed, it's actively encouraged. At IDEO, we achieve this by creating maker spaces that offer people the right environment, materials, and tools to bring their ideas to life. We have brainstorm kits that include Post-its and Sharpies in every meeting room, signaling to participants that they should feel free to express themselves in a variety of ways. Employees are also invited to create their own work environments. For example, in our New York office, where I'm based, we all came together to design our "phone booths," or rooms for private calls, each themed after a famous New

Yorker (such as Woody Allen and Robert De Niro). We have "tour stops"—areas to bring visitors so they can get a sense of what our people create and care about. And we're constantly trying to find ways to turn the mundane into the engaging. One ritual is to insert elaborate animated GIFs into office-wide emails, so that they have a narrative, build community, and encourage dialogue.

A Common Purpose, Tailored

IDEO's purpose statement—"Positive and disproportionate impact in the world through design"—is ambitious and intentionally broad. On its own, it might inspire the people working in our studios around the world, but it probably isn't quite enough to help them connect the dots to their work. (*How do I have positive and disproportionate impact? Where do I begin? Are my interests and passions the same as IDEO's?*) That's why we also ask our locations to tailor IDEO's purpose to their particular markets or studios. For example, in China, a localized purpose statement might be something like "Creating new value for the country by enabling enlightened leaders to tackle systemic challenges," while in London it might be "Enabling organizations to deliver on and exceed their promises to people." And in a larger office, like San Francisco, each part of the business might create its own purpose statement, such as the food and beverage studio's "Bridging the worlds of culinary and science to solve the world's food problems." This helps employees figure out which work best aligns with their skills and where they're going to be most engaged and successful in the organization.

A Social Contract

You might have heard about the *Little Book of IDEO*. In it, we talk about seven common values that bind us together: be optimistic, collaborate, learn from failure, embrace ambiguity, talk less and do more, take ownership, and lastly, make others successful. These values are, in fact, the behaviors that drive our social contract. They allow teams to govern themselves without needing lots of oversight and management, and they help people understand what success looks like. We've found that they are also a great aid in development. The employees we hire rarely struggle with the skills of their jobs, but sometimes they do need support in adhering to these values.

Bottom-Up Innovation

Top-down directives don't work terribly well at IDEO. We've learned that the best new ideas and capabilities are often incubated from the bottom up through someone's personal energy and commitment. For example, one of our fastest-growing businesses focuses on education. Sandy Speicher, the managing director at IDEO who leads that work, grew a team of 23 people with projects across the world because she believed that her passion—education—was something that IDEO should also care about. When leaders want to initiate a project, we always explain the underlying need and give a clear sense of the desired outcome so that people get aligned around a common goal. The best strategies are ones that people can make their own.

In a world where great talent is hard to find and harder to retain, companies succeed by keeping their employees engaged, happy, and fulfilled. There is no silver bullet. But these four principles have helped IDEO go a long way in achieving that goal.

Duane Bray is head of global talent and a partner at IDEO.

Index

absenteeism, 2
accountability, 137–138
acquiescence bias, 23
Aguinis, Herman, 183
Ahearne, Michael, 59–70
altruism, 147–151
Amabile, Teresa, 79–103
ambiguity, in survey questions, 24–25
ambition, 107–108
American Institute of Stress, 218
Anderson, Diana Newton, 142
Apple, 89–90
Aristotle project, 161
Association of Accounting Technicians, 205–206, 219
Assurance, 193–194
Augustin, Sally, 233–239
autonomy, 5
    burnout and, 191
    citizenship behaviors and, 126
    decision making and, 43
    innovation and, 244
    in meaningful work, 108–109
    promoting, 48–49
    psychological need for, 48–49
    in supporting progress, 92–95
    trust and, 108–109
    workplace design and, 238
availability bias, 12
Awakening Compassion at Work (Dutton), 206
Awbery Management Centre, 180
Awethu Project, 207
Azagba, Sunday, 218

badge systems, 158–159
Bapat, Vivek, 145–154
Baumgartner, Natalie, 6, 71–75
behavioral norms, 96–97
beliefs, self-limiting, 164
belonging, 5
beneficiaries, interaction with, 114–116
benefits, 36
    engagement and, 3
    most desirable, 37–39, 235–236
Berg, Justin, 146
Berlin, Johann, 236
Beyond Performance Management (Hope and Player), 41

biases
  acquiescence, 23
  in assignments of B players, 163–164
  availability, 12
  false-consensus, 72–73
  against flexible work schedules, 225–231
  social desirability, 22–23
Birdi, Kamal, 222
Blair-Loy, Mary, 228
blame, 219
Bolam, J. Paul, 117
Bolino, Mark C., 125–129
bonuses, 39–40. *See also* reward systems
brainstorm kits, 242–243
Bray, Duane, 241–245
brownout, 122
Buckingham, Marcus, 42–43
Buell, Ryan, 114
burnout
  brownout and, 122
  case study on avoiding, 193–194
  demands/resources and, 178–184
  effects of, 186
  focusing on what matters and, 186–187
  grunt work and, 209–213
  in highly engaged employees, 175–184
  loneliness and, 203–208
  the right amount of stress and, 195–202
  in stars, 180–183
  tips for fighting on teams, 190–192
  warning signs of, 190

cabdrivers, 67
Cacioppo, John, 204
calendar fragmentation, 15
Camerer, Colin, 67
Cameron, Kim, 206, 217–223
Cappelli, Peter, 154
career goals, 155–160
career myth, 156–157, 160
career traps, 157
Carucci, Ron, 53–58
catalysts, 84–85, 92–95, 100
Cave, John, 139–140
C-DOT, 213
Cech, Erin, 225–232
Center for American Progress, 218
challenges
  bias in assigning, 163–164
  employee satisfaction from, 44–45
  stress levels and, 200–201
  stretch assignments, 168–169
  unlocking passion and, 122
Chamorro-Premuzic, Tomas, 105–110
checking in versus checking up, 98
Children's Hospital of Philadelphia, 170
citizenship behaviors, 125–129
citizenship crafting, 127–129
coaching, 133–138
  stress levels and, 197–198
Cohen, Jordan, 155–160
collaboration, 75, 162
  metrics on, 13
  workplace design and, 234, 237
color, in workplace design, 237–238

commissions, 67–68

communication

about flexible work schedules, 228, 230–231

in citizenship crafting, 127–128

in employee development, 169–170

in employee happiness, 28–31

encouraging people to talk about problems, 221–222

insincere, 53–54, 54–56

psychological drives and, 51

remote, tools for, 229–230

in supporting progress, 93

in support of growth and development, 134–136

true-north conversations, 146–147

community, 192

compassion, 206

competence, psychological drive for, 49–50

compliments, 141

confidence, modeling, 201–202

consequences, 199

context, for gratitude, 57

core performers, 60, 61–64

creativity, 196

inner work life and, 81–83

job crafting for, 152–154

Crick, Francis, 80

Cullen, Jennifer, 21–25

culture

always-on, 188

of engagement, 241–245

hiring for fit with, 108

of hospitality, 111–113

at IDEO, 241–245

of inclusion and empathy, 206

positive, productivity and, 217–223

sales, 70

curiosity, 107

customers

communicating changes in priorities of, 93

loss of interest in working with, 18

showing employees how they're helping, 114–116

cutthroat environments, 217–218

CVS, 142

dashboard tools, 15

Davey, Liane, 186–194, 195–202

David, Susan, 1–8, 54, 219

Deci, Edward, 48

decision making, empowerment for, 43

Deloitte, 119

demands, burnout and, 178–184

development. *See* growth and development

developmental alliances, 136–137

discretionary effort, 12

disengagement, 53–58, 179

costs of, 2, 218

loneliness and, 205

distractions, 187–188, 237

DNA model, 79–80

double-barrel questions, 24

Double Helix, The (Watson), 79–80

double negatives, 24

drive-by praise, 54–55

Dutton, Jane, 146, 206, 221

Dweck, Carol, 148–150

"Easy Way to Make Your Employees Happier, An" (Wiseman), 44
Edmondson, Amy, 221–222
email, 188, 189
Emotion Revolution in the Workplace (study), 177
emotions, 86, 201–202
    workplace design and, 234
    See also inner work lives
empathy, 206, 220–221
"Employee Experience, The," 235
employees
    decision-making rights for, 43
    engaged-exhausted, 177
    happiness of, 28–31
    helping move on, 123
    recognition of, 42–43
Employment Confidence Survey, 37
empowerment, 43, 222
engaged-exhausted workers, 177
engagement
    of B players, 161–165
    burnout and, 175–184
    definition of, 3
    extrinsic versus intrinsic rewards and, 35–45
    factors involved in, 19
    flourishing and, 176–178
    Gallup survey on, 11–12, 27
    at IDEO, 241–245
    impact of, 11–12, 176
    individualized approach to, 6–8, 71–75
    influence from colleagues and, 14
    levels of, 1–2
    measuring, 11–20
    monitoring and improving, 29–31

progress principle and, 79–103
psychological drives and, 50
relationships and, 14–15
research on, 5–6
responsibility for, 3–4
results of measuring, 15–19
self-perceived versus actual, 12–13
smart, 183–184
surveys, problems with, 12, 21–25
workplace design and, 233–239
work schedules and, 15
entitlement, 126, 210
environmental psychology, 234
ethics, 36, 39–40
exasperation, 141
exhaustion, 203–204
experimentation, 159–160, 242–243
extra-role behaviors, 125–129
extrinsic rewards, 35–40

Faas Foundation, 177
fairness, 40–41
false-consensus bias, 72–73
familiarity, disengagement from, 117–118
Families & Work Institute, 226–227
family life, 28–29, 30. *See also* flexibility
feedback, 19
    positive, stress levels and, 199–200
    progress loop and, 99–102
    recognition, 42–43
financial incentives. *See* reward systems

Finkelstein, Sydney, 123
fixed mindset, 148. *See also*
        mindset
flexibility, 6, 225–232
    growth mindset versus,
        148–149
    work schedule, 37, 38, 39
flourishing, 176–178
Fowler, Susan, 47–52
Fractl, 37
framing, 113, 117
Fuller, Ryan, 11–20
Future Workplace, 235

Gallup, 1–2, 11–12, 27, 54, 176,
        205
GameStop, 28–31
Gardner, Timothy M., 16–18
Garrad, Lewis, 105–110
General Social Survey, 203
Gerstenblatt, Brett, 142
Gino, Francesca, 114–116
Give and Take (Grant), 222
Glassdoor, 37
goals
    for big thinkers, 151–152
    career, 155–160
    catalysts and, 92–95
    developmental, 136–137
    engagement as, 4
    inspiring people to work
        toward, 121
    for learning, 50
    minor milestones, 88–89
    promoting autonomy around,
        48
    stretch, 179
    values alignment with, 49
    See also progress
        principle

Google, 37, 161
Grant, Adam, 128, 222
Green, Paul, 115
Greenleaf, Robert, 120
Grenny, Joseph, 111–118
growth and development
    accountability for, 137–138
    of B players, 161–165
    of competence, 50
    flex work and, 225–232
    job personalization and,
        145–154
    mentoring, career goals, and,
        155–160
    networks for, 206–207
    personalization of, 74–75
    relatedness and, 49
    restarting, 167–171
growth mindset, 147, 148–150.
        See also mindset
grunt work, 209–213
guilt gratitude, 55–56

habit, 196
Haidt, Jonathan, 221
Handmaker, Steven, 193–194
handwashing in hospitals, 117
happiness
    asking employees about, 27–31
    challenging work and, 44–45
    complacency from, 109
    inner work life and, 81–83
    loneliness and, 205–206
Happiness Track, The (Seppala
        and King), 204
health, 106, 207, 218, 235–236
health insurance, 37, 38, 39
Hedge, Alan, 235–236
helping, 221
hierarchy of needs, 47–48

Hocking, Shanna, 170
Hofmann, Dave, 114
Hom, Peter W., 16–18
Home Depot, 43
Hope, Jeremy, 41
"How Google Sold Its Engineers
    on Management," 134
"How to Prioritize Your Work
    When Your Manager
    Doesn't" (Su), 122
hygiene factors, 3–4

IBM, 74–75
IDEO, 241–245
impression management, 22
inclusion, 206
individuality
    approach to engagement and,
        6–8
    of B players, 162–163
    citizenship behaviors and,
        127–129
    customization versus catering
        to and, 153
    development and, 74–75
    job crafting based on,
        108–109, 145–154
    in motivators, 71–75
    purpose and, 243
    recognition and, 42–43
    rewards tailored for, 41–42
    salesforce compensation and,
        60–70
    values and, 72–73
inertia, 196
inhibitors, 85, 93–95, 101
inner work lives, 81–83
    managers and, 96–97
    minor milestones and, 88–89
    power of progress and, 83–87
    progress loop and, 99–102

innovation
    bottom-up, 244
    small wins in driving,
        79–103
inquisitiveness, 107
insincerity, 53–56
inspiration, 220
integrity, 220
intrinsic rewards, 40–42

Jobs, Steve, 89–90
job crafting, 108–109, 127,
        145–154
    for creatives, 152–154
    establishing goals in, 151–152
job descriptions, 145–146
job fit, 163
Johnson, Whitney, 139–140,
        167–171, 209–213
Jones, Kerry, 37–39

Kaplan, Robert, 120
Kappes, Heather Barry, 107
Kawashima, Jim, 42–43
Kelley, David, 242
Kibler, Michael E., 122
King, Marissa, 203–208
Kislik, Liz, 161–165
Klotz, Anthony C., 125–129
Knightsbridge Human Capital,
        186
Kohn, Alfie, 36, 39
Koloc, Nathaniel, 229–231
Kotter, John, 196
Kramer, Steve, 79–103

laggards, 60, 64–66
leaders and leadership
    avoiding burnout and, 189

checking in with employees
by, 28–31
in creating meaningful work,
105–110
empathy in, 220–221
giving permission for,
164–165
knowing your people, 73–74
moral purpose and, 112
motivation based on psychological drives and, 50–51
personality characteristics of,
106–109
in positive climate creation,
221–222
recognition by, 54–58
servant, 120–121
learning
burnout and, 191–192
challenging work and, 44–45
manager coaching to support,
133–138
new skills, 169–170
setting goals for, 50
LifeLabs Learning, 156
lighting, 235–236
Lim, Noah, 68
LinkedIn, 189
listening, 135
Little Book of IDEO, 244
loneliness, 203–208
effects of, 204–205
*Loneliness: Human Nature and
the Need for Social Connection* (Cacioppo), 204
loyalty, 218
Luna, Tania, 155–160

management
applying the right amount of
pressure in, 195–202

catalyst/nourisher use by,
93–95
coaching to support learning
by, 133–138
in creating meaningful work,
90
destroying meaningful work,
91–93
flex work and, 230
inner work life and, 81–87
in job crafting, 146
motivation as job of, 1–8
quality and time investment,
measuring, 13–14
recognition by, 42–43, 54–58
in supporting progress, 95–99
targeted support by, 97
"man on the bench" effect,
65–66
Maslow, Abraham, 47–48
McKenna-Doyle, Michelle, 140
meaningful work, 7–8
benefits of, 106
contextualizing recognition
and, 57
discovering work that excites
and, 119–124
going beyond the job and,
125–129
grunt work and, 209–213
in helping customers, 114–116
how managers strip meaning
from, 91–93
innovation and small wins in,
79–103
leaders in creating, 105–110
positive culture and, 220
progress as, 80–103
relatedness and, 49
storytelling in, 111–118
stress and, 198–199
for teams, 186–187

meaningful work (*continued*)
understanding your work as,
106–110
meetings, 188, 193
participation metrics, 13
Meister, Jean C., 235–236
mentors and mentoring, 74–75,
128, 155–160
metrics
influence from colleagues, 14
management quality and time
investment, 13–14
performance curve, 69–70
what to measure, 11–20
on work schedules, 15
Meyer, Danny, 111–113
micromanaging, 108
milestones, 158–159
mindset
citizenship crafting and, 127
in creating meaningful work,
105
fixed, 148
growth, 147, 148–150
servant leader, 120–121
Misra, Sanjog, 67
mission
loss of enthusiasm about, 17
passion and, 120
mission moments, 117–118
mission statements, 149–150
modeling, 201–202, 212–213,
230
Moeller, Julia, 175–184
mood, 84, 234
moral purpose, 112
Morgenstern, Julie, 186, 187,
188, 189
Mosow, Julie, 185–194
motivation
checking in with employees
about, 28–31

choice in, 54
extrinsic versus intrinsic,
35–45
to go beyond the job, 125–129
inner work life and, 86
loss of, as warning sign of quitting, 17
as a manager's job, 1–8
motivators
autonomy, 43
challenge, 44
disengagement and, 53–58
extrinsic versus intrinsic,
35–45
individual differences in, 6,
71–75
inner work life, 81–83
intrinsic rewards, 40–42
psychological drives, 47–52
recognition, 42–43, 53–58
reward systems, 35–45
for salespeople, 59–70

Naas, Clifford, 186
Nair, Harikesh, 67
National Football League,
139–140
Nelson, Bob, 42–43
networks
developmental, 206–207
managers', quality and breadth
of, 14
metrics on, 13, 14–15
New Economics Foundation,
207
norms, 96–97, 193
nourishers, 84–85, 92–95, 100

O'Boyle, Ernest, 183
observation, 142–143

O'Connor, Lindsey Trimble, 225–232
O. C. Tanner Learning Group, 54
Oettingen, Gabriele, 107
Ophir, Eyal, 186
optimism, 107, 212
outdoor views, 235–236
ownership, 91–92

Parent, Daniel, 28–31
Parker, Pam, 170
passion, 119–124, 128
people analytics, 12–20
PepsiCo, 89–90
perceptions, in inner work life, 81–83, 86–87
performance
  consequences for poor, 199
  curve, shifting upward, 69–70
  extrinsic versus intrinsic rewards and, 35
  grunt work and, 209–213
  inner work life and, 81–83
  pressure for, 49
  progress loop and, 99–102
  promoting autonomy and, 49
  recognition and, 54–55
  reward systems and, 39–40
personal needs, 30, 179
  exhaustion and, 203–204
  flex time and, 226–231
  loneliness and, 203–208
  See also family life
Pitroda, Sam, 213
place design, 233–239
play, 242–243
Player, Steve, 41
Plummer, Matt, 180–183
Podsakoff, Nathan, 125
positive culture/climate, 96–97, 212, 217–223

Positive Leadership (Cameron), 206
"Power of Dignity in the Workplace, The" (Valcour), 43
praise, drive-by, 54–55
Pressman, Sarah, 204, 220
priorities, 122
  work time, 193–194
prize structures, 62–64, 68. *See also* reward systems
productive range of distress, 196
productivity, 11–12
  of high performers, 183
  loneliness and, 205–206
  loss of as sign of quitting, 16
  positive work cultures and, 217–223
profitability, 2, 11–12
progress principle, 80–103
  catalysts and nourishers in supporting, 92–95
  daily checklist for, 100–102
  definition of, 80–81
  in development, 137
  in meaningful work, 89–92
  minor milestones and, 88–89
  power of, 83–87
  progress loop and, 99–102
  setbacks and, 85–86
psychological drives, 47–52
  autonomy, 48–49
  competence, 49–50
  relatedness, 49
purpose, 187, 243
  leaders in creating, 112
  psychological need for, 49

questions
  about career goals, 157, 159
  about employee happiness, 30
  about workplace design, 238

questions (*continued*)
  ambiguous, 24–25
  on career goals, 159
  in coaching, 135–136
  to discover employees' pas-
    sions, 121–122
  double-barrel, 24
  to encourage experimentation,
    159–160
  to identify strengths, 141–143
  for promoting development,
    50
  on surveys, 22–25
  on transferable skills, 158
  "we" versus "I," 23
quitting, signs of impending,
  16–18

recognition, 42–43
  of B players, 162–163
  burnout and, 191
  of collective successes, 207
  contextualizing, 57
  disengagement from lack of,
    54–58
  as goal, 4
  growth mindset and, 149
  guilt gratitude, 55–56
  making stuff up, 55
  in meaningful work, 91–93
  of personal sacrifice, 57
  of strengths, 142–143
relatedness, 49
relationships
  building with employees, 30
  burnout and, 203–208
  coaching and, 138
  crafting, 127
  with customers, 114–116
  engagement and, 14–15

fostering, 220
  metrics on, 13, 14–15
  positive culture and, 220
  social contract and, 244
  storytelling in encouraging,
    113
  strong-tie and weak-tie,
    14–15
Reschly, Amy L., 176
resilience, 206
resources
  burnout and access to, 178–184
  to leverage strengths, 74–75
  managers as, 98
  supporting progress with,
    92–95
respect, 220
rest, 188, 190–191
retention
  of B players, 161–165
  checking employee happiness
    and, 30–31
  costs of replacing employees
    and, 218
  helping someone move on
    and, 123
  job crafting and, 154
  recognition and, 54
  reward systems and, 36
  signs that someone is about to
    quit and, 16–18
reward systems
  commissions, 67–68
  cutthroat environments and,
    219
  fair approach to, 40–41
  grunt work and, 211–212
  individualization in, 60–70
  intrinsic versus external re-
    wards, 40–45
  meaningful work and, 105–106

most desirable benefits and,
37–39
pace-setting bonuses, 64–65
prize structures, 62–64
promoting autonomy and,
48–49
recognition, 42–43
for salespeople, 59–70
tailored to individuals, 41–42
Rimm, Allison, 27–31
rituals, 207
Robert Half Management Resources, 57
roles
altruistic, 151
conflict between, 28–29
extra-role behaviors,
125–129
suited to strengths, 139–143
*Rookie Smarts: Why Learning
Beats Knowing in the New
Game of Work* (Wiseman),
44
Ryan, Richard, 128

safety
cutthroat environments and,
218
environment of, survey design
and, 25
workplace, 48
workplace design and,
238–239
salespeople, 59–70
core performers, 60, 61–64
laggards, 60, 64–66
multi-tier targets for, 61–62
natural social pressure on,
65–66
performance curve for, 69–70

prize structures for, 62–64
program-induced social pressure on, 66
stars, 60, 66–68
stress levels for, 197–202
SAP India, 168–169
SAS, 37
Sculley, John, 89–90
"Secrets of the Superbosses"
(Finkelstein), 123
self-determination theory, 48
Seppala, Emma, 175–184,
203–208, 217–223, 236
servant leadership, 120–121
setbacks, 85–86, 101
Shake Shack, 111–113
Sharaf, Mesbah, 218
Shetty, Sumeet, 168–169
skills
encouraging employees to
learn, 169–170
mentoring for development
of, 74–75
transferable, 158
Smith, A. David, 117
social contract, 244
social desirability bias, 22–23
social pressure, 65–66
Staats, Brad, 115
stars, 60, 66–68, 162
burnout in, 180–183
State of the American Workplace
(report), 1, 27, 54, 205
Steenburgh, Thomas, 59–70
stimulating work, 6. *See also*
meaningful work
storytelling, 111–118
recognition and, 56
strengths
of B players, 162–163
citizenship crafting and, 128

strengths (*continued*)
  identifying team member,
    141–143
  leveraging, 74–75
  why talented people don't use
    their, 139–143
stress
  assessing levels of, 196–197
  citizenship crafting and, 128
  coaching and, 197–198
  confidence and, 201–202
  cutthroat environments and,
    218
  dealing with problems and,
    200–201
  engagement and, 177–184
  inner work life and, 82–83
  meaningful work and,
    198–199
  positive feedback and,
    199–200
  pressure to perform and, 49
  the right amount of, 195–202
  See also burnout
Stress in America (report), 207
stretch assignments, 168–169.
    See also challenges
Su, Amy Jen, 119–124
surveys, 2
  availability bias in, 12
  on employee happiness,
    27–31
  engagement, 12
  on most desirable employee
    benefits, 37–39
  problems with, 21–25

talent pipeline, 65–66
task crafting, 127

teams
  avoiding burnout in,
    185–194
  B players in, 161–165
  fair approach to financial
    incentives with, 40–41
  management time spent
    with, 14
time management, 15
  burnout and, 179
  grunt work and, 210–213
toxins, 85, 94, 101
transferable skills, 158
transparency, 213
true-north conversations,
  146–147
trust, 43, 220
  leader's ability to, 108–109
turnover, 2
"Turn the Job You Have into
    the Job You Want" (Wrzes-
    niewski, Berg, and Dutton),
    146

Union Square Hospitality Group
  (USHG), 111–113

vacation time, 37, 38, 39
Valcour, Monique, 43, 133–138,
  189, 190–192
values
  altruism, 147–151
  developing, 49
  hiring for, 108
  at IDEO, 244
  individual differences in,
    72–75
Van Knippenberg, Daan, 221

VitalSmarts, 117–118
VoloMetrix, 15–16

Wagner, Anthony, 186
Walgreens, 42–43
Watson, James, 79–80
Weight Watchers (WW), 156
Weiner, Jeff, 189
Weinstein, Netta, 128
well-being, 29, 219–223
Wharton, Amy, 228
"What Great Managers Do"
    (Buckingham), 42–43
What You're Really Meant to Do
    (Kaplan), 120
"When Helping Helps" (Wein-
    stein and Ryan), 128
"Why Incentive Plans Cannot
    Work" (Kohn), 36

wins, small, 79–103
Wiseman, Liz, 44
workloads, editing, 187, 190
workplace conditions, 48
workplace design, 233–239
work schedules
    avoiding burnout with,
        186–188
    flexible, 37, 38, 39, 225–232
    metrics on, 15
    personal life and, 179
    well-being and, 219
Wrzesniewski, Amy, 146
WW (Weight Watchers), 156

Yale Center for Emotional Intel-
    ligence, 177
Yam, Kai Chi, 126
You First (Davey), 186

Harvard Business Review

Invaluable insights
always at your fingertips

With an All-Access subscription to
Harvard Business Review, you'll get
so much more than a magazine.

Exclusive online content and tools
you can put to use today

My Library, your personal workspace for sharing,
saving, and organizing HBR.org articles and tools

Unlimited access to more than 4,000 articles in the
Harvard Business Review archive

Subscribe today at hbr.org/subnow